“Fraud is occurring on an increasing scale—its prevention and timely detection has never been more important. Dr Sandeep Goel beautifully documents an organization’s commitment to implementing robust mechanisms to identify, assessment, and mitigate potential fraudulent risks. It draws upon in-depth knowledge and skills to manage an effective and robust risk management framework across businesses.”

—**Mr. Sanjeev Bikhchandani,** *Founder and Executive Vice Chairman, Info Edge, New Delhi*

“The global trend for stronger facilitation in key business and trade areas is the genesis for an equally strong risk management system. Dr Sandeep Goel, in his lucid style, brings forth the typical attributes and assessments of frauds and makes the reader become aware about the regulatory aspects of fraud management in his new book. An asset for all Businesses.”

—**Dr. Kavita Bhatnagar (IRS),** *Additional Director General, National Academy of Customs, Indirect Taxes & Narcotics (NACIN), Ministry of Finance, GoI, Bhopal*

Fraud Risk Management

This book presents and investigates the potential and inherent fraud threats to an organization. It helps develop a programme to detect and prevent them by way of a fraud risk management system. The author analyses global corporate explosions and experiences through the implementation of fraud management techniques for future learnings. The case studies comprise the likes of Enron, WorldCom, Parmalat, Satyam, Lehman Brothers, the IL&FS, and the recent Silicon Valley Bank.

The volume covers the following:

- Fraud Risk Assessment: Types, Framework & The Triangle
- Fraud Detection and Prevention: External & Internal risks and Financial Statements' Frauds
- Fraud Risk Governance: Fraud Management Practices & Corporate Governance Mechanism
- Fraud Resistance System: Fiduciary System for "shareholders' value"

Thoroughly updated to reflect contemporary global trends and real-world corporate cases, the book will be indispensable to individuals, corporate executives, and management students. It will also be a useful tool for executive and management development programmes (EDPs and MDPs). Financial professionals and anyone looking for a quick refresher on corporate fraud and governance will find it a worthy resource.

Sandeep Goel is Senior Professor of Accounting and Finance, and Corporate Governance at Management Development Institute (MDI), Gurgaon, India. He holds two doctorates, one in Finance;

and another in Accounting from the Faculty of Management Studies, University of Delhi. He completed his bachelor's with Hons. and master's degrees in Commerce with specialization in Finance from Shri Ram College of Commerce, and the Department of Commerce, Delhi School of Economics, University of Delhi, respectively. He has three decades of industry and academic experience across various organizations and institutions of repute, including the Shri Ram Group, the University of Delhi, and MDI Gurgaon. He sits as Independent Director on the Board of Machino Plastics Ltd., Gurugram, a Suzuki JV. He is Visiting Professor to the Faculty of Management, University of Lodz, Poland, and Aix-Marseille Graduate School of Management—IAE AIX-Marseille University, France. He is Management Trainer and Consultant to organizations like Maruti Suzuki, Canara Bank, JK Tyre, PFRDA, NPCI, IRS, ITS, FIA Business School (Brazil), Bata, Encore, Federal-Mogul Goetze (India) Ltd., SOS Village International, Cairns India, National Banking Institute (Nepal), Druk Holdings (Bhutan), UltraTech Cements, ONGC, and many more. He is a prolific writer and has authored more than 15 books and published over 100 research articles and cases in national and international journals of repute. He has been conferred with the Award for Excellence in Teaching, 2023–24, 2015–16, and the Award for Excellence in Research, 2015–16 at MDI.

Foundations of Finance

Series author: **Sandeep Goel** is a Senior Professor of Accounting and Finance, and Corporate Governance, Management Development Institute (MDI) Gurgaon, India.

This series presents the foundations of financial knowledge in a lucid and accessible format. The books in the series deal with critical themes in financial literacy and proficiency today, such as financial accounting, cost accounting, corporate finance, contemporary finance, forensic accounting, fraud analytics, and fraud risk management. Each volume in the series deals with updated expert insights, current global trends, and real-world cases in finance and is richly illustrated with tables, figures, and learning tools. The individual books in the series will be indispensable for individuals, business managers, and management students pursuing undergraduate and postgraduate courses in finance. They will also be important resources for executive and management development programmes (EDPs & MDPs) as well as beginners and professionals interested in a short refresher course on finance and financial management.

Fraud Risk Management
Sandeep Goel

Fraud Risk Management

Sandeep Goel

Routledge
Taylor & Francis Group
LONDON AND NEW YORK

Designed cover image: Getty Images

First published 2026
by Routledge
4 Park Square, Milton Park, Abingdon, Oxon OX14 4RN

and by Routledge
605 Third Avenue, New York, NY 10158

Routledge is an imprint of the Taylor & Francis Group, an informa business

British Library Cataloguing-in-Publication Data
A catalogue record for this book is available from the British Library

ISBN: 978-1-041-21222-5 (hbk)
ISBN: 978-1-041-22021-3 (pbk)
ISBN: 978-1-003-73022-4 (ebk)

DOI: 10.4324/9781003730224

Typeset in Sabon
by Deanta Global Publishing Services, Chennai, India

Contents

Figures

Tables

Preface

The world has seen evidence of multiple corporate frauds over the years. This calls for extensive fraud risk management. In our modern-day risk landscape, companies must navigate uncertainties in the internal and external environment.

According to the Association of Certified Fraud Examiners' (ACFE) Report to the Nations 2024, organizations around the world lose an estimated 5% of their revenue to fraud each year. Fraud risk management, simply put, is the process of assessing fraud risks within your organization and then developing an anti-fraud programme that stops any fraudulent activity before it happens. Having a reputation for integrity is crucial to safeguarding market confidence and public trust. If there is no fraud risk management strategy in place, fraud has the potential to grow like a virus, destroying the health of businesses and causing greater and greater losses.

An examination into the fraud risks for company by size, location, and industry will aid its anti-fraud initiatives and lead to best practices for minimizing fraud losses. The absence of control mechanisms or overriding of the existing ones account for more than half of corporate frauds. The current book provides a comprehensive analysis of contemporary frauds and helps implement effective methods for identifying and mitigating them. Most significantly, it will make it possible for investors and stakeholders to use it as an efficient tool for financial investment, monitoring, analysis, and resource allocation. Easy readability with helpful instructional cases and examples comprehends the fundamental organizational structure, topical coverage, and presentation of the book. I hope that these enhanced features will offer increased value to the book and users at large.

Organization of the book

The book has been divided into eight chapters. It has been logically sequenced to facilitate better connectivity and learning among the readers. Most chapters are self-contained and can be read independently of the others.

Chapter 1, "The fraud framework," provides an overview of the conceptual perspective of fraud and its motivational triangle.

Chapter 2, "Fraud: Types, schemes, and preventives," explains different forms of frauds conducted by business organizations with precautionary measures taken to stop fraud.

Chapter 3, "Fraud risk management: Concept, process, and system," discusses the rationale of the fraud management system, its process, and essential factors of its effective implementation, including the 4Ts approach.

Chapter 4, "Corporate governance: The essence of fraud risk management," explains governance principles, regulation, and metrics to design sound management practices.

Chapter 5, "Management compensation: Economic value added (EVA)," provides an overview of value-based management compensation for sound corporate governance.

Chapter 6, "Industry interface of fraud risk management structure," deliberates on fraud management in sectors like BFSI (banking, financial services and insurance) and public. It also covers the "who," "how," and "where" of fraud risk management.

Chapter 7, "Global frauds," delves into the prominent corporate fiascos and collapses at the world level.

Chapter 8, "Brainstorming," decodes risk-governance chart governance and fraud models like Benford's law, and case studies for hands-on simulation.

The book will help you develop your fraud detection and management territory, which is crucial for your professional success and career advancement. This is the ideal synthesis of theory and practice. The effort is to maintain a lucid style yet comprehensive in approach. I sincerely hope that the quality and presentation of this book will make it genuinely valuable to the readers. Any constructive comments and suggestions for future improvement of the book are highly appreciated and welcome at *sandeepgoel1810@gmail.com*.

Happy learning!

Acknowledgements

This book is the culmination of decades of extensive experience imparting fraud risk management knowledge and skills to thousands of participants and students at various corporate and organizational levels. I would like to take this opportunity to thank everyone whose thought-provoking questions and inquiries inspired me to write this one-window volume on the subject.

I wish to thank God Almighty for everything in life! The work would be incomplete if I did not acknowledge my parents' contribution. They have been a constant source of inspiration for me and have always stood by me through thick and thin. My wife provided her unstinting support and encouragement in completing the book. My daughter Maanya is my soul, whose smile always keeps me going in life.

I am also thankful to the entire team of Routledge, New Delhi, including Dr Shashank Sinha, Mr. Yogesh Srivastava, and Ms. Anvitaa Bajaj for their tremendous support and wholehearted cooperation at all stages of publication of this book.

My sincere thanks are also due to Mr Sanjeev Bikhchandani and Dr Kavita Bhatnagar for their valuable support and endorsements of the book.

Last but not least, I sincerely express my gratitude to the following fellow academic colleagues and professional associates for providing their invaluable advice and inputs for the enrichment of the book:

- **Dr Brian P. Miller,** *Professor of Accounting, Warrington College of Business, University of Florida, US*
- **Dr Robert C. Rickards,** *Professor of Accounting, German Police University, Münster, Germany*

- **Dr Maciej Turała,** *Vice Dean for International Relations, University of Lodz, Poland*
- **Mr S.S. Sharma,** *IAS Retd, Former Secretary, Government of India, Gurugram*
- **Dr J. P. Singh,** *Former Professor of Finance, Department of Management Studies, Indian Institute of Technology, Roorke*
- **Mr Aditya Jindal,** *Chairman cum Managing Director, Machino Plastics Ltd., Gurugram*
- **Dr Niti Nandini Chatnani,** *Professor of Finance, Indian Institute of Foreign Trade, New Delhi*
- **Dr Sonam Chawla,** *Associate Professor of Organizational Behaviour, O.P. Jindal Global University, Sonipat*
- **Dr Vishakha Bansal,** *Assistant Professor of Finance & Control, Indian Institute of Management, Shillong*
- **Dr Ajay Kumar,** *Assistant Professor, Bharati Vidyapeeth Institute of Management & Research, New Delhi*

Abbreviations

AAS	Auditing and Assurance Standard
ACFE	Association of Certified Fraud Examiners
AML	Anti Money Laundering
ATO	Account Takeover
BFSI	Banking, Financial Services and Insurance
CAG	Comptroller and Auditor General of India
CBDC	Central Bank Digital Currency
CBI	Central Bureau of Investigation
CII	Confederation of Indian Industry
COCE	Cost of Capital Employed
COSO	Committee of Sponsoring Organizations of the Treadway Commission
CSR	Corporate Social Responsibility
CVC	Central Vigilance Commission
DCA	Department of Company Affairs
DHFL	Dewan Housing Finance Ltd.
ED	Enforcement Directorate
EPS	Earnings Per Share
ESG	Environmental, Social, and Governance
EVA	Economic Value Added
EWS	Early Warning Signals
FCO	Fraud Control Officer
FDI	Foreign Direct Investment
FEMA	Foreign Exchange Management Act
FRMC	Fraud Risk Management Committee
FTC	Federal Trade Commission
HUL	Hindustan Unilever Limited
ICAI	The Institute of Chartered Accountants of India
IL&FS	Infrastructure Leasing & Finance Services Limited

JIP	Japan Industrial Partners
LC	Letter of Credit
LODR	Listing Obligations and Disclosure Requirements
MCA	Ministry of Corporate Affairs
MVA	Market Value Added
NOPAT	Net Operating Profit After Tax
OECD	Organisation for Economic Co-operation and Development
P2P	Peer-To-Peer
PAT	Profit After Tax
PII	Personally identifiable information
PNB	Punjab National Bank
RBI	Reserve Bank of India
SEBI	Securities and Exchange Board of India
SFIO	Serious Fraud Investigation Office
SOX	Sarbanes–Oxley Act
SPE	Special Purpose Entities
SVB	Silicon Valley Bank
SWIFT	Society for Worldwide Interbank Financial Telecommunication
WACC	Weighted Average Cost of Capital

1 The fraud framework

Corporate fraud and misconduct remain a constant threat to public trust and confidence in the corporate functioning and financial system of the country. Public sector organizations are also exposed to fraud, particularly in service delivery and the supply chain. Therefore, it is essential to have an overview of fraud and misconduct risk management and keep a close watch on its fundamentals. It shall provide organizations with a road map to go beyond a check-box approach to managing the risks of fraud and misappropriation, and instead develop, put into practice, and assess proactive measures that top organizations have found to be effective.

Fraud—The definition!

Fraud is "an intentional deception that causes the personal or some form of gain of an employee or an entity." It is any dishonest action done to gain an unfair advantage or make an unlawful profit. This illegal act benefits the perpetrator while harming other people.

> *Fraud becomes a crime when it is a "knowing misrepresentation of the truth or concealment of a material fact to induce another to act to his or her detriment."*

For instance, it is fraud when an employee takes money out of the business register and uses it for himself. This would be advantageous to the employee at the cost of the business and through unlawful means.

DOI: 10.4324/9781003730224-1

> "Corporate fraud" happens when top executives of large corporations commit fraud; it frequently has a billion-dollar scope. Investors, creditors, consumers or clients, other firms, and ultimately the crime's originating company and its staff are the victims of corporate fraud. When the scam is finally discovered, the perpetrating company is frequently left in ruins and is obliged to file for bankruptcy.

A significant portion of the money stolen unlawfully through corporate fraud is frequently never retrieved since the offenders would have already spent it.

Definition of fraud under various legislations

A. As per **Section 17 of the Indian Contract Act, 1872,**[1] "Fraud" means and includes any of the following acts committed by a party to a contract, or with his connivance, or by his agent, with intent to deceive another party thereto or his agent, or to induce him to enter into the contract:

1. the suggestion, as a fact, of that which is not true, by one who does not believe it to be true;
2. the active concealment of a fact by one having knowledge or belief of the fact;
3. a promise made without any intention of performing it;
4. any other act fitted to deceive;
5. any such act or omission as the law specially declares to be fraudulent.

Explanation—Mere silence as to facts likely to affect the willingness of a person to enter into a contract is not fraud, unless the circumstances of the case are such that, regard being had to them, it is the duty of the person keeping silence to speak, or unless his silence is, in itself, equivalent to speech.

Illustrations:

(a) A sells, by auction, to B, a horse which A knows to be unsound. A says nothing to B about the horse's unsoundness. This is not fraud by A.

(b) B is A's daughter and has just come of age. Here the relation between the parties would make it A's duty to tell B if the horse is unsound.
(c) B says to A—"If you do not deny it, I shall assume that the horse is sound". A says nothing. Here, A's silence is equivalent to speech.
(d) A and B, being traders, enter into a contract. A has private information of a change in prices which would affect B's willingness to proceed with the contract. A is not bound to inform B.

B. **Section 447 of the Companies Act, 2013**[2] provides for the definition of fraud and also the punishment for committing it. As per this section, "Fraud" in relation to the affairs of a company or body corporate includes "any act, omission, concealment of any fact, or abuse of position committed by any person or any other person with the connivance in any manner, with intent to deceive, to gain undue advantage from, or to injure the interests of the company or its shareholders or its creditors or any other person, whether or not there is any wrongful gain or loss."
wrongful gain or wrongful loss."

> "Wrongful gain" is defined as gain by unlawful means of property to which the person gaining is not legally entitled. Similarly, "wrongful loss" is defined as loss by unlawful means of property to which the person losing is legally entitled.

Therefore, to fall within the meaning of fraud, the following should have happened:

1. acts, omissions, concealment of fact or abuse of position should have taken place;
2. such acts, omissions, concealment of fact or abuse of position should have the essence of *mens rea* in them; and
3. irrespective of whether or not they resulted in "wrongful gain" or "wrongful loss".

Fraud conceptual framework

A business is an independent legal entity that is established by a statute or a registration process. It is independent of the obligations and rights of its shareholders. Some of these businesses operate as corporate organizations.

> *A business is treated as a separate legal body distinct from its owners. It can be defined as an association of individuals for a common object and has no strict legal or technical significance.*

It is a top priority for every nation to establish some sort of accountability and regulation for these businesses. In a nutshell, the "respondeat superior" theory is the concept of criminal corporate liability that was transferred from tort law to criminal law. This doctrine states that if an organization's agents act within the bounds of their apparent or actual authority, the organization may be held criminally liable and guilty for any illegal actions taken by those agents.

Real authority is the authority that a firm has fully granted to its agent or employee; *Apparent authority* is the authority that a reasonable citizen can infer from an agent. Thus, the company may be held criminally responsible for the actions of the employee if a reasonable relationship between his or her criminal activity and his or her corporate duties can be identified.

According to the current legal framework, there are crimes that constitute serious frauds for which mandatory prison sentences are the recommended punishment, even when committed by a corporate body. For violations of such acts, the corporation may be subject to fines and legal action. The corporation is liable for the actions of others since it is a legal person.

Fraud is one of the biggest risks to the viability and sustainability of any organization. It can cause far more harm than just financial losses or legal infractions. It could seriously harm businesses, undermining the brands' connections and reputation that are essential to the company's continued growth and success.

The economy and stakeholders are significantly impacted by the prevalence of corporate fraud. Corporate fraud has become an unavoidable aspect of the average person's daily life and poses a severe threat to the economy as a whole. The interests of all parties involved are negatively impacted, particularly investors who lose out on their hard-earned money. Any corporate fraud that occurs in the country has an impact on the capital market at large.

Punishment for fraud: Without prejudice to any liability including repayment of any debt under this Act or any other law for the time being in force, any person who is found to be guilty of fraud shall be punishable with imprisonment for a term, usually not less than six months but which may extend to ten years or so, and shall also be liable to a fine which shall not be less than the amount involved in the fraud but which may extend to three times the amount involved in the fraud. Where the fraud in question involves public interest, the term of imprisonment shall not be less than three years.

Prevention of fraud: Under Section 211, the Central Government has set up an office called "Serious Fraud Investigation Office" (SFIO) to investigate corporate frauds. After a case has been assigned to SFIO, no other investigating agency may continue the investigation into the offence under the Act. If the SFIO has reason to suspect someone of a crime based on the evidence with them, they have the authority to make an arrest. The SFIO shall submit a report to the Central Government upon the conclusion of the investigation. The Central Government may direct the SFIO to initiate prosecution against the company. Further, the Central Government can order an investigation into the affairs of a company upon the receipt of a report of the Registrar or inspector; upon intimation of a special resolution passed by a company that the affairs of the company ought to be investigated; or in the public interest.

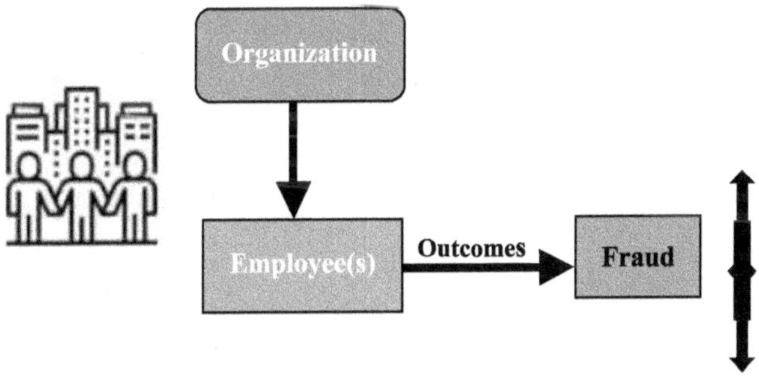

Figure 1.1 Fraud chart

> *As presented in Figure 1, this idea holds that fraud is not random; rather, it happens when the circumstances are right for the fraudster. It produces illicit profit or incentive or relieves the person or thing under unwanted pressure. This increases the want to act in such a way and provides a sense of increased control without considering the repercussions.*

What is fraud triangle?

The fraud triangle is a concept that explains why employees commit fraud in the workplace. It explains the motivation(s) behind an individual's or corporation's decision to commit fraud and consists of three elements responsible for fraud—*pressure, rationalization, and opportunity*.

> *According to this theory, as is illustrated in Figure 1.2, fraud occurs when the conditions are ideal for a perpetrator with*

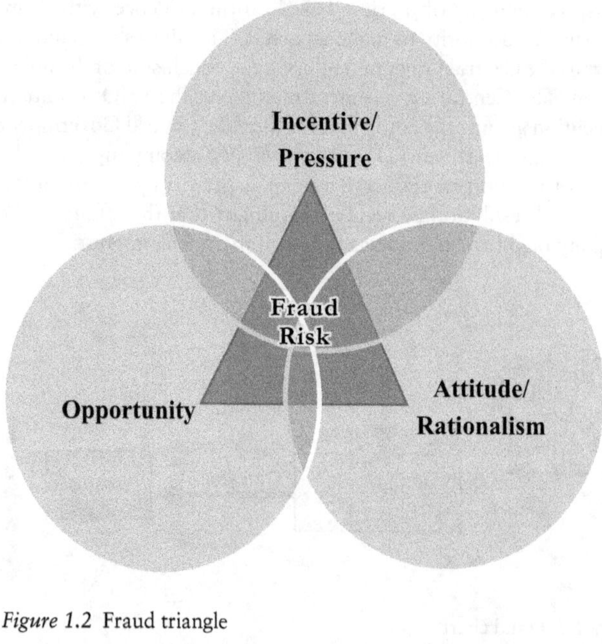

Figure 1.2 Fraud triangle

inherent motives. It releases the subject of unwelcome pressure, generates illegitimate profit, or is an attitudinal issue, or may be a combination of all. This gives the impression of reasons for committing frauds, as discussed below.

Motivations for frauds

The main components of the fraud triangle model are listed below.

1. Pressure

Pressure, alternatively called incentive, refers to an employee's mindset towards committing fraud.

One of the driving forces behind fraud is pressure, which can be from superiors or from personal financial reasons. The potential for the fraud triangle is encouraged and motivated by both of these pressures. If legal and reasonable measures are not taken to relieve the pressure, people may turn to irrational measures. Common personal financial pressures include unresolvable financial problems like *not having enough money, pressure from banks to pay back loans, and maintaining one's standard of living.*

Although there are other types of pressure that can lead to fraud, the need or desire to attract and retain investors is the most important. In the highly competitive global business environment of today, these are potential causes. A common element of corporate fraud schemes that seek to artificially increase a company's perceived profitability is the use of fraudulent accounting techniques. These tactics are motivated by the perceived need to maintain investor satisfaction.

Thus, cases of incentive-led fraud can be classified as follows:

1 *Personal gains or greed.* The need to pay personal expenses, the ambition to earn more money, a gambling addiction, etc., are examples of personal motivators.
2 *Bonuses.* Sales and net income are two common financial indicators used to evaluate an employee's performance. Bonuses based on financial metrics put pressure on employees

to meet targets, which may cause them to commit fraud to meet the goal.

3 *Investors' sentiment and analyst expectations.* Pressure to commit fraud may arise from the necessity to meet or outperform the expectations of analysts and investors in order to maintain or increase stock prices.

Example: Enron

The Enron scandal is one of the most well-known cases of corporate deception due to the aforementioned pressurizing factors. Enron, a significant energy corporation, was making billions upon billions of dollars in earnings at its peak. However, when the company began to face debt problems and declining revenues, business executives used widespread accounting fraud to hide the truth.

Both Enron and its accounting firm, Arthur Andersen, ultimately failed. While thousands of employees lost their jobs, Enron's investors and creditors lost billions of dollars.

The *Sarbanes-Oxley Act (SOX)* was passed because of the Enron accounting scandal, requiring more transparency in financial reporting and stricter penalties for any company found to have engaged in accounting fraud.

2. *Opportunity*

Opportunity refers to circumstances that make it possible for fraud to occur. It is the only component over which a business has complete control.

Employees may look for an opportunity to steal when under pressure. They might be able to steal goods and resell them on the open market if the inventory system is not subject to internal control. One way to achieve this is through an abuse of position; for instance, when a superior coerces a subordinate into providing window dressing for an account.

Corporate fraud is often motivated by greed, the same motivation that drives most frauds. It arises in the following situations:

(i) *Inadequate internal controls*—Internal controls are implemented to ensure that accounting and financial data are accurate. Weak internal controls, such as insufficient job division, supervision, and process documentation, create opportunities for fraud.

(ii) *Weak top management*—The "tone at the top" refers to the commitment of the board of directors and upper management to maintaining moral values, honesty, and integrity; a company with a weak tone at the top is more susceptible to fraud.

(iii) *Insufficient accounting processes*—The recording in the financial statements is done as per the corporation's accounting policies. Inadequate accounting practices could provide employees with a chance to manipulate the numbers.

3. *Rationalization*

Rationalization refers to an individual's justification for committing fraud. Justification is the last stage in the fraud triangle theory.

Fraudsters must give a plausible explanation for their behaviour. Instead of considering themselves criminals, most fraudsters explain the circumstances that led to their actions. Similarly, performance and shareholder pressure for dividends and other things can be explained by managerial fraud.

The following are some examples of common justifications used by fraudsters:

- "Mistreatment." A person may harbour resentment towards their employer or supervisor and believe that defrauding others is a way to get even if they believe that their boss is mistreating them.
- "Management involvement." If the upper management is found to be involved in the act of fraud, then the workforce may decide to follow in the footsteps of people in higher positions within the company if there is a weak tone at the top.
- "No way out." Someone may believe that they risk losing everything, including their job, if they don't commit fraud. Fraudulent actions may result from the belief that there is no other option.

Frauds: The global outlook...

Corporate fraud has been a major concern globally over the past few decades, and India is no exception. Among the most common fraudulent crimes are cash embezzlement and misappropriation, insider trading, accounting fraud, breach of trust, intellectual property theft, and others. In response to this threat, the governments of the respective nations have enacted laws and regulations to prevent corporate fraud and have put in place a number of policies and procedures to ensure the safety of the general public. Every organization, whether business or non-business, needs an efficient "fraud risk management" system in order to achieve rational results and make proper use of valuable resources. Organizations run a higher risk of losing millions or even billions due to fraudulent activities if they don't have adequate risk management and fraud prevention procedures in place.

Fraud is a global phenomenon and is now prevalent online. According to the Federal Trade Commission (FTC), consumer fraud reports increased by 70% in 2021 compared to 2020, when the majority of people were cooped up indoors due to the pandemic. Consumers lost a total of $5.8 billion, mostly to impostor scams and online shopping scams. The Association of Certified Fraud Examiners' (ACFE's) 2022 Global Fraud Survey reported that the average business loses about 5% of its revenue to occupational fraud every year. The median cost of each fraud case was $117K, with some heavy outliers that pulled the average cost to $1,783,000 per fraud case. The industries most at risk of *internal* fraud are real estate and wholesale trade, while the industries most at risk of *external* fraud include e-commerce and insurance. However, fraud is not limited to any one industry. Every business is vulnerable.[3]

Frauds in India

The fraud incidents in India are being severely pumped up by the pervasive and systemic corruption in society. The rise in corporate fraud in India has been attributed to a number of factors, but the most significant ones are the lack of due diligence procedures, internal control, and strict enforcement of the law, which lead to unethical business practices. In the 2001 Ketan Parekh scam, which cost 12,000 crore rupees (INR), the convicted offender, Parekh, stole bank funds and used them to invest a sizeable amount in a number of businesses. After a trial, Parekh was immediately arrested and sentenced to a year of rigorous incarceration.

The Indian Parliament has passed several rules and regulations, including the Companies Act, 2013 and the "Prevention of Money Laundering Act, 2002," to combat corporate fraud. To further guarantee the safety and security of depositors' money, the Reserve Bank of India and the Indian government have implemented strict laws and procedures for banks.

As mentioned earlier, additionally the Indian government has established a dedicated investigation mechanism to promote increased financial transparency in its fight against corporate crime in the form of a body called the Serious Fraud Investigation Office (SFIO).

Corporate frauds are still very much a problem in India, despite government efforts to stop it. The main cause of this is the widespread and institutionalized corruption in Indian society. Therefore, a lot of aggressive steps must be taken to prevent corporate fraud, and ongoing efforts must be made to stop it, solve the problem, and fortify the country's financial system. Strengthening government laws and their enforcement, along with raising public awareness, will be necessary to reduce and eventually eradicate corporate fraud in India.

Fraud: Focal areas

As organizations do their best to formulate a comprehensive, proactive strategy to prevent, detect, and respond to integrity threats, they can be well served by focusing their efforts upon:

- identifying and understanding the risks of fraud and misconduct that could jeopardize increasingly intricate and international business objectives;
- assessing the operational efficacy and design of corporate compliance programmes and related anti-fraud programmes and controls;
- adhering to anti-fraud and governance standards issued by reputable standard-setters;

- gaining knowledge about more effective ways to design and assess controls to prevent, detect, and respond to fraud and misconduct;
- reducing exposure to corporate liability, sanctions, and litigation that may result from legal or stakeholder expectations;
- deriving value from compliance investments by establishing a sustainable process for risk management and performance enhancement; and
- achieving high levels of business integrity through sound corporate governance, internal control, and transparency.

Fraud perpetrators

The big question arises—who commits fraud? There are different types of fraudsters, and they usually fall into one of three categories:

1. Pre-planned fraudsters—They have the intention of committing fraud from the start. These can range from short-term offenders, who make widespread use of stolen plastic cards, credit or debit cards and fraudulent social security numbers, to longer-term offenders, such as bankruptcy fraudsters and those who carry out intricate money laundering schemes.
2. Intermediate fraudsters—They are initially truthful but switch to fraud when things get tough or due to life circumstances that alter their typical behaviour, like not getting the due promotion or having to pay for a family member's care.
3. Slippery-slope fraudsters—Those who merely continue trading even though they are objectively unable to settle their debts. This is applicable to both major businesspeople and regular traders.

References

1. https://indiankanoon.org/doc/299780/ (accessed on 11 May, 2024)
2. https://www.mca.gov.in/Ministry/pdf/CompaniesAct2013.pdf (accessed on 11 May, 2024)
3. https://datadome.co/threats/fraud-risk-management/#:~:text=Effective%20Risk%20Management-,What%20is%20fraud%20risk%20management%3F,external%20fraud%20for%20an%20organization

2 Fraud

Types, schemes, and preventives

Fraudsters are constantly thinking up ways to get access to your financial and personal information to cheat you or your account. You need to arm yourself with the codes and processes of these scams to protect yourself. All stakeholders need to understand the various types of frauds committed in today's business world to safeguard their assets and maintain their hard-earned wealth—particularly as new avenues for fraud and illicit activities continue to unfold. There is a continuing need to explore the best practices to detect and prevent these sophisticated manipulations.

Corporate "external" fraud

This type of fraud arises from outside of an organization, commonly involving vendors, customers, or competitors. External fraud may also involve individuals, groups, organized crime, and even terrorist groups.

External fraud may occur along with other forms of fraud. For instance, vendor fraud might also involve a corrupt employee in an organization's purchasing department (occupational fraud).

The main forms of external fraud include vendor fraud, customer fraud, and competitor fraud.

- **Vendor fraud** is common when an organization doesn't have a good procurement system or a voucher system and doesn't inspect all items coming into its receiving department. A lot of businesses lack these kinds of internal controls, which can affect the inventory movement and which can have a significant impact on the reporting of the financial statements. There are three typical ways that vendor fraud can happen:

DOI: 10.4324/9781003730224-2

    - *Short-shipments*: Orders that are dispatched partially or not at all, but are nonetheless charged for a complete shipment.
    - *Balance billing*: The vendor can overcharge or fail to reimburse a returned shipment using this billing method by just charging the "balance on the account."
    - *Substandard goods*: When a seller bills for a product but provides one that is of lower quality.
- **Customer fraud** can occur in multiple ways. Customers may defraud an organization through the manipulation of accounts receivable and returns of goods. An example of returns would be when an individual orders an item online and later returns a different or lower quality item for full credit. This is very common in e-commerce trade.
- **Competitor fraud** is highlighted by two prevalent schemes: theft of confidential data and sabotage. Information theft is a multifaceted crime that is included in the category of corporate intelligence theft. Competitors can use many techniques which are difficult to detect. Sabotage involves the intentional destruction or damage of the business to prevent it from working properly. Investigating these kinds of cases tends to require assistance from counter-intelligence specialists.

These three external fraud categories are summarized in Figure 2.1.

Figure 2.1 Types of external fraud

Corporate "internal" fraud

Internal fraud or "occupational fraud" is fraud committed by an organization's employees. This kind of fraud can be put mainly into the following categories: asset misappropriation, corruption, financial statement fraud, and others.

Although there is no typical profile of a fraudster in this area, evidence shows the presence of factors, like pressure and incentives, which, on average, are responsible for the fraudster's behaviour.

Internal fraud includes employees undertaking any of the following actions:

- **Asset misappropriation** is the most common form of occupational fraud but the least costly on average. It occurs when an employee improperly uses an employer's asset for personal use. It can be "monetary" or "non-monetary." The monetary type is when the employee borrows or misuses money for personal reasons. Common cash theft is the simplest form of asset misappropriation, that is, theft of cash or stock from the company's resources or theft from other employees. Employees or staff of the company may be involved in the theft of assets like properties or inventory to gain financial benefits.

In addition to this simple monetary form, more sophisticated ways of asset misappropriation of non-monetary nature may occur in three areas of an organization: its revenue cycle, expenditure cycle, and production cycle.

- *Revenue cycle fraud (cash receipts)*: examples include sales skimming, theft of cash or cheques, and improper credit approval.
- *Expenditure cycle fraud (cash disbursements)*: examples include improper purchases, payroll fraud, and improper payments.
- *Production cycle fraud*: examples include payroll and inventory fraud (claiming more hours than actually worked; theft of raw materials and finished goods).

Fake sales/purchases and inventory shrinkage are some of the examples of asset misappropriation fraud of a non-monetary nature.

There are numerous other frauds of an internal nature which can impact any organization in the absence of proper controls. Examples include fraudulent use of company cheques, improper guarantees to customers, and so on. With the increasing use of technology, new schemes continue to emerge. Identification of a perpetrator may be difficult or impossible if digital information is subject to inadequate accounting controls.

- **Corruption** is the second most common type of occupational fraud. It is a form of dishonest or fraudulent conduct by those in power. The main form of corruption consists of an individual exercising their undue influence upon others. Examples of this form are conflicts of interest, bribery, improper gratuities, and economic extortion. Corruption is mostly seen in bid rigging and kickback cases. Your employees can steal from your business in several ways. The most common scams are embezzlement and misappropriation of funds. Generally, white-collar crimes occur when employees have financial power without oversight and control.

It may also manifest as "counterfeiting." This is a type of fraud incident that can have serious and severe financial repercussions for the company. The fraudsters can create realistic-looking materials and packaging by using new and modern technology, which allows them to deceive legitimate traders, such as wholesalers and retailers. For the fraudster, counterfeiting is a profitable business activity that offers countless opportunities to use technology to generate significant commercial profits. It is an issue that impacts many different industries, such as fashion, electronics, and pharmaceuticals. Nevertheless, such fraud frequently affects a large number of victims, not just the company that has been tricked or had its reputation abused.

> Authorities responsible for investigating corruption are
>
> - Central Vigilance Commission (CVC),
> - Comptroller and Auditor General of India (CAG),
> - Serious Fraud Investigation Office (SFIO),
> - Central Bureau of Investigation (CBI),
> - Anti-Corruption Bureau,
> - Lokpal (Central Level) and Lok Ayukta (State Level), and
> - Enforcement Directorate (ED).

- **Financial statement fraud** occurs when an individual manipulates an organization's financial statements. It involves fudging important numbers like sales, revenues, assets, and liabilities. Usually, this is done to dupe investors or the public, manipulate stock, or increase bonuses.

This kind of fraud not only damages the company, but it also damages lenders, shareholders, and others who rely on financial statements to make decisions. Financial statement fraud is usually perpetrated by senior managers.

On average, financial statement fraud is the costliest form of internal fraud and technically not confined to internal boundaries. Reasons for manipulating financial statements range from poor company performance to greed, and it appears where an opportunity is present. The most common form of financial statement fraud is manipulating profits—"earnings management."

The internal fraud types are presented in Figure 2.2.

There are numerous forms of internal frauds that may have an impact on small enterprises, though large-scale enterprises are not an exception.

- **Workman's compensation fraud**

Workman's compensation insurance is something that many small firms provide to their employees in case they are injured at work. Regrettably, some workers take advantage of the system to

Figure 2.2 Types of internal fraud

benefit themselves. Workers sometimes fabricate claims for exaggerated or fictitious work-related injuries. A person may report an injury to their employer in order to file a claim under their workman's compensation policy if they are hurt on their own time during off-peak hours. In other situations, employees will report that they were hurt on the job, and an old injury will resurface. As a result, these employees remain jobless, and their insurance provider covers their medical costs. To help stop these scams, make sure your employees are working in a safe environment and have access to all the safety equipment they need to complete a task.

- **Cheque tampering**

Another type of fraud that economic crime investigation experts advise small businesses to learn about is cheque tampering. The most evident type of cheque tampering fraud is when an employee forges cheques to fictitious payees and then colludes with those people or businesses to steal the money. Another way cheque tampering occurs is when an employee tampers with legitimate cheques to change the payee's name to their own name, a fake name, or a shell company set up to collect the fraudulent payments. To prevent cheque tampering fraud, make sure the owner of the company personally signs each cheque and has several people confirm the company's financial information.

- **Revenue skimming**

Revenue skimming is a type of fraud that most commonly takes place when cash is given by customers at a business. This fraud occurs when customers pay cash for an item or service. The cashier just has to make sure the customer does not receive a receipt. The employee takes the cash from the customer and keeps it for himself; since there is no paper trail, there is no record of the item or service being sold. Businesses that engage in cash sales should divide and rotate employee responsibilities to prevent revenue skimming.

- **Fraudulent invoicing**

Economic crime investigation professionals alert small businesses about fraudulent invoicing schemes. In this scheme, a person or business will send a professionally constructed invoice for products or services that were never purchased. Companies sometimes pay these bills without considering or verifying that the purchase was made. In order to steal money from the company, the fraudster—typically a sales or accounting employee—creates fictitious invoices.

As some businesses choose to pay these fictitious invoices, the trickster on the other side of the scam succeeds. To prevent falling victim to a fraudulent invoicing scam, make sure to thoroughly review every invoice you receive and compare it to the goods or services you have already purchased.

- **Payroll fraud**

Unfortunately, payroll fraud makes up a fair percentage of occupational fraud worldwide. Small businesses have a high risk of falling victim to payroll fraud, as most do not have anti-fraud controls in place. As a result, it is increasingly important for small businesses to be aware of this type of fraud. Payroll fraud can present itself in many different ways. For example, an hourly wage worker might claim to have put in more hours than they actually did in order to receive payment for hours they did not work. Payroll fraud can also happen when salaried workers alter their salaries and have access to payroll records. It is also possible when a commissioned worker reports fictitious orders or sales. Some might even go so far as to have a coworker clock in and out for them in order to falsify their attendance records.

According to most studies, payroll fraud disproportionately affects small businesses because they are less likely to have anti-fraud measures and systems. In order to prevent payroll fraud, economic crime investigation experts suggest having supervisors or managers review timesheets on a regular basis.

- **Vendor billing fraud**

Vendor billing fraud occurs when an employee creates a shell company and pays the business with company cheques from their workplace. Examples of fraud that can mimic vendor billing include fraudulent invoicing and cheque tampering.

Two warning signs to watch out for are cheques payable to cash or a business listing the same address as an employee's home. Another form of vendor fraud is hiring a friend or relative who runs their own business to supply goods or services. In order to benefit from their relationship, the small business employee might be complicit in the friend or family member's overcharging. One way to avoid vendor billing is to review each vendor before paying them.

To reduce occupational fraud, an organization should have regular monitoring, internal and external audits, reconciliations, physical inspections, and awareness of its risks and internal weaknesses. The best strategies to prevent internal fraud are to hire reliable staff and have the owner personally check all bills, invoices, and timesheets including human resources. For instance, make sure to regularly check the criminal histories and references of potential hires. These additional procedures may prove to be beneficial even though they can take a lot of time and effort.

Financial statements fraud (Accounting fraud): Variants

Fraud related to financial statements of a corporate can hit you in several ways and is "internal" in form, as discussed above. These frauds are widespread today; therefore, their variants are discussed specifically in this section.

Accounting fraud

Accounting frauds are of a financial nature and internal in approach. They involve purposely altering a company's financial documents to distort its financial position.

A good percentage of businesses engage in accounting misconduct each year. In the current economic climate, filled with escalating costs and uncertainties, the risk of accounting fraud continues to be high. Usually, the likelihood of accounting fraud increases when companies are under pressure to achieve specific goals. Therefore, it is crucial for shareholders and other stakeholders to be knowledgeable about accounting fraud and detecting deceptive accounting practices.

Typical accounting fraud practices could be categorized as:

(i) Recognizing revenue on false grounds
(ii) "Secret" reserves
(iii) Capitalization of expense
(iv) Off-balance sheet items

1. *Recognizing false revenue*

These days, companies operate in extremely high-pressure environments wherein investors will not overlook a company's inability to meet goals. Many institutions have been hence forced to engage in revenue-manipulation exercises out of the fear of not being able to meet market expectations.

Earnings-manipulation techniques in this context range from slightly delaying the year-end shipping date to engaging in fraudulent financial reporting by means of fictitious sales. A business may be tempted to recognize paper revenue that does not occur in actuality. With this practice, a company bills the paper customer and holds materials on its behalf, with the entire attendant costs attributed to the seller's account. There could also be mixing of non-core receipts with regular revenue by the corporation just to meet some numbers. These would be a flagrant violation of generally accepted accounting principles. All these practices result in the creation of higher profits in accounting periods.

So, companies accelerating the recording of revenues to give a nice look to their operating results while being in desperate need of financing or meeting market reactions is universal.

2. *Secret reserves*

Frauds in accounting can be practised either by smoothing earnings to help sustain the firms' earnings stream ex-ante or by managing earnings upwards to achieve earnings increases ex-post. Such earnings trickery sneaks through grey areas of sensitive and subjective accounting estimates such as reserves and provisions in the profit and loss account and balance sheet. One of the smoothing practices is ad-hoc creation or revocation of the discretionary debt reserve accounting estimate.

The Economist (2010) states, "Dell was found by SEC maintaining '... reserves' using Intel's money. According to SEC, Dell would have missed the earnings forecast done by the analysts in every quarter between 2002 and 2006. This included a deal with Intel, a big microchip-maker. Under the deal, Dell had agreed to use Intel's central processing unit chips exclusively in its computers for which the payments were not disclosed. This leads to a penalty of $100 m for Dell."[1]

3. *Capitalization of expense*

The corporation calling revenue expenses as capital expenses and reporting them as fixed assets in the balance sheet is another common way of accounting manipulation. Items like *research and development costs* and *miscellaneous expenses* are at the discretion of the management to record them as assets instead of expenses in financial statements. This ultimately results in an increase in the size of the net worth of the company.

This is a very common practice, violating the accounting principles of a "business entity." A business owner uses business assets for personal use, presuming they are his own. An accountant treats the use of business goods for personal needs as a drawing which is an implied loan to the owner. It must be paid back to the business. But usually, these corporate mispractices are deliberately overlooked in financial reporting. According to the Report to the Nation on Occupational Fraud and Abuse (ACFE, 2008), asset misappropriation can be classified into different schemes, such as: *skimming, cash larceny, fraudulent disbursements, and noncash larceny and misuse.*[2]

4. *Off-balance sheet items*

Hiding the transactions in the name of "contingent liabilities" and not showing them in the main balance sheet is a practice often used to cover up debt obligations and guarantees given on behalf of subsidiary concerns.

The above treatment leads to erosion of profits for the business in the later periods and affects the shareholders' wealth creation in the long run.

So, an insight into how managers can manipulate earnings is essential for all market participants for better financial decision-making. Knowing what tricks managers have up their sleeve can help market participants unravel the effects of any manipulation and, in the long run, blunt the effectiveness of earnings management techniques. The role of standard setters and financial practitioners in this regard is undoubtedly significant. *At WorldCom, officers and employees cut company line costs with "improper releases from reserve accounts" as part of its overall $9 billion overstatement of income from 1999 through the first quarter of 2002, according to the SEC.*[3]

Societal fraud

There are frauds that are beyond the above categorization of corporate or an organization. Their outreach is to society at large. Here are some common types of fraud you should be aware of as a common person:

1. *Identity theft*

Identity theft refers to any kind of fraud committed by stealing personal information. An identity thief uses your personally identifiable information (PII)—such as your name, birthday, etc.—to gain access to your accounts and assets. It can lead to credit, bank, or loan fraud. An identity thief can drain your bank account, take new loans in your name, or run up your credit card.

Criminals have a few options when it comes to stealing your sensitive information. They might target you with a "phishing attack" where they email, call, or text pretending to be from your bank. Or, they could target you with a cyber-attack to get you to install malware on your devices that steals your logins and passwords. They might even steal your mail or illegally change your address to get your credit card statements sent to them.

Hackers have stolen billions of pieces of information in recent years alone through data breaches. So even if you haven't been directly targeted by a criminal, there's a good chance you're still vulnerable to financial fraud.

2. *Mortgage fraud*

Mortgage fraud is a wilful misrepresentation or omission of facts by an individual or an organization, such as overstating the ability to repay a loan or any such material information, which leads the bankers and lenders to approve the loan on false grounds or to relax the terms and conditions of the loan such as the interest rate or the repayment schedule. This fraud falls under a criminal offence.

These *mortgage fraud cases* have plagued the insurance and loan industry more than most other types of fraud. Such frauds were on the rise during the 2000s, leading to the 2007–08 housing bubble. Mortgage fraud could happen to mortgage loans bought for securitization or held in an enterprise's own portfolios. Fraud can occur during the loan origination, underwriting, closing, or while a loan is being serviced on an enterprise's behalf.

The categories of mortgage fraud are "fraud for profit" and "fraud for housing."

(i) *Fraud for profit* is called "income fraud." It involves a scheme where the fraudster makes money through the fraud.

In order to have a mortgage loan approved, borrowers may fabricate their identity, place of employment, or income. Parties involved in loan originations that might fabricate collateral, breach contracts, or embezzle money include appraisers, attorneys, and title agencies. Sellers of mortgage loans may misrepresent underwriting requirements or offer a single mortgage loan multiple times. Servicers have the ability to move funds—whether custodial or otherwise—to accounts they use for their own benefit.

(ii) *Fraud for housing* is the "occupancy fraud." In this instance, the borrower falsely informs the lender that he requires the loan in order to buy a home for his own use. The true motivation, meanwhile, is to resell the same item when it is available at a higher price. As such, it is an investment as opposed to a requirement. In these situations, there's a chance he won't be able to pay back the loan if it's not paid off in full and the new buyer receives possession. Consequently, by failing to disclose the true purpose for taking out the loan, the principal borrower commits the fraud.

3. *Tax fraud*

Tax evasion fraud is the deliberate use of wrong information in filing income tax returns. It is an illegal act where a person or an entity wilfully tries to evade tax liability. Defaulters take advantage of the tax system and violate laws.

This unlawful act causes significant loss to the governments' income. Most defaulters are either huge business entities or affluent individuals. Unlike *tax evasion,* there are legitimate ways of minimizing the tax burden within the law. This is referred to as *tax avoidance.*

"Tax evasion" is fraudulent tax practice where a taxpayer adopts illegal measures from refraining his tax liability. "Tax avoidance" is a legal way of reducing the tax payable, given the deductions applicable to taxpayers. It helps reduce the tax burden of individuals and businesses, including major corporates.

There are two methods that the Income Tax Department uses to handle these types of scams. In the event of a civil fraud, the tax liability is reevaluated and the defaulter is subject to civil penalties in addition to the outstanding tax balance. On the other hand, in cases of criminal fraud, the defaulter is prosecuted in addition to paying a financial penalty. It's possible that this will result in his imprisonment.

"Tax refund fraud" occurs as most people get stressed when dealing with their taxes or the Income Tax Department. This makes tax-related matters an appealing target for financial scams.

One of the most common forms is tax refund fraud. In such frauds, criminals fraudulently file tax returns in your name. They report incorrect income in order to maximize your refund, which the criminal will then deposit into their own account.

In another type of case, a fraudster pretends to be a tax official and demands personal information or payment for taxes owed. Or, you may deal with an unethical tax preparer who steals your information or fraudulently files for a refund under your name by not accepting these phony offers.

4. *Plastic card fraud*

There are several ways that criminals can steal your credit card information. They could steal your physical card, trick you into entering information on a phishing website or email, buy your details from some e-source, or use any number of other credit card scams.

One of the worst types of fraud to clean up is when a thief gets access to your bank account or card number(s). It is criminal behaviour when a burglar obtains your bank account or debit or credit card number. Hackers may also create a clone of your physical card using just your debit/credit card numbers. These may result in suspicious transactions on your credit card or bank statement, unfamiliar charges on your account, or even fraud alerts from your bank, credit card issuer, or credit monitoring service.

Plastic money fraud may occur if either the physical card or the card number is stolen. If you're a victim, contact the fraud department of your card issuer, bank, or financial institution and explain the situation. They'll be able to help you freeze or close your accounts and get new cards.

5. *Advance fee fraud*

Advance fee fraud is when a thief requires you to send money in advance for payments, products, or services. The promised rewards can range from better credit to money from a foreign company, and more. But in the end, they either aren't what was promised or never arrive.

One common example is a scammer claiming to get you a better deal on a loan in return for a "finder's fee." They'll ask you to sign a contract that requires you to pay the fee once they introduce you to the financing source. But after you pay, you'll often discover it isn't what the "finder" claimed it to be, or worse, that you're ineligible for the loan and since you signed the contract, you have no recourse.

Be wary of any offer that seems too good to be true or that only accepts unusual payment methods, like wire transfers or gift cards. Only share financial information once you're sure a process is legitimate.

6. *Fake cheque fraud*

The cheque fraud is a simple bank scam that relies on the fact that it can take quite a while for the cheque to be verified. Fraudsters will wait outside the bank or send you a picture of a cheque and ask you to deposit it for them. Then, they'll tell you to keep some of the money for yourself and send them the rest. When the cheque bounces a few days later, the money will be taken out of your account.

It can also be asking you to deposit a cheque for them and wire them the money (minus a fee). If you've deposited a cashier's cheque and sent the scammer a wire transfer, there unfortunately isn't a way to get your money back.

7. *Financial account takeovers*

When an identity thief scams you online to gain access to one of your online financial accounts (or any account), it's known as an "account takeover" (ATO). A recent study showed that millions of consumers had been victims of account takeovers.

"Bank account takeover" can happen pretty easily just by someone stealing a cheque out of your mailbox, getting a hold of your account info through an email scam, or (in some extreme cases) using malware to gain access to all of your personal information.

So, this kind of scam works through phishing, a data breach, or an emerging cyber threat where they steal your credentials while using public Wi-Fi. A thief can buy goods with access to your Amazon account or employ social engine techniques to ask your friends for money.

8. *Ponzi scheme fraud*

Simply put, this is an investment fraud which gets you to put money into an investment that isn't real. While we often imagine predatory structures, the most common fraud schemes are simple: the thief disappears with your money.

Fraudsters often lure victims with promises of large gains, little risk, and once-in-a-lifetime opportunities. In many cases, investment schemes target affinity groups—such as people who share a common religion or cultural background—to build trust. Sometimes the supposed investors are asked to sign non-disclosure agreements, which can keep victims quiet once the thieves disappear.

9. *Fraudulent charities*

Scammers use philanthropy as fraud, too. Charity fraud entails creating a fake charity and collecting "donations" that disappear along with the thief—like "military veteran charities"—that sound like ones you know and trust.

They will make you believe and claim that you're a previous donor when you know you've never sent them money. Before donating, check their sites and never share information such as your bank account number when you can use another payment method.

Fraud preventive measures

Financial fraud can be devastating. Whether a scammer gets access to your internal financial data as an employee or credit card numbers or convinces you to invest in a fraudulent scheme, you have lost your hard-earned money. The various challenges of the "fraud triangle model" (as discussed in Chapter 1) and the means required to control them are given below:

1. *Screening of new hires*

It's wise to do more than just background checks and reference checks on new hires for your company, particularly if you're hiring financial professionals—accountants who will be handling sensitive financial data. Even for a small business, having a rigorous hiring process can help reduce fraud. Any employees who handle money transfers, bank account information, or other sensitive data should have their backgrounds checked thoroughly.

2. *Strong internal controls*

There needs to be strong internal control, legal compliance, and strict consequences for fraud in order to stop businesses and management from committing fraud. Preventive internal controls need to be put in place because they aid in preventing accounting errors and inconsistencies from happening in the first place. They further help an organization detect frauds faster and experience fewer frauds overall.

These may consist of:

1. Separation of responsibilities, meaning no one person is in charge of a complete financial transaction;
2. Controlled access to the accounting system;
3. Expense verification;
4. Limited access to assets, such as cash, equipment, or inventory.

These controls, like conducting routine inventory counts, internal audits, and reconciliations, can help confirm that fraudulent behaviour isn't having an impact on your business.

3. *Financial checks and balances*

Perform an internal review of your company's finances at regular intervals—this could be a month or a week. This may entail examining significant differences between estimates and actuals, validating vendor orders, searching for missing paperwork, and matching payments to invoices. Conducting special audits or hiring a third party to do so will help in preventing fraud and may even discourage future fraudulent activity.

4. *Sound information technology and online systems*

The platforms that your staff members frequently utilize, such as emails, ERPs, and accounting software, present a significant risk for fraud. Limit the number of staff members who can access the system at first, as more users may increase the risk of fraud or data breaches.

Moreover, spend money on anti-virus software, firewalls, and staff education on phishing scam prevention. You can protect yourself from having critical information disclosed by even mandating that staff members verify email addresses twice before replying.

5. *Favourable employee policies*

The employee policies must be favourable so that they can approach the management in need and can get finance and the required help from the company instead of committing fraud.

6. *Training employees*

Employees in departments like accounting or human resources that are vulnerable to fraud should receive training on how to spot red flags and take preventive measures. Contrary to popular belief, employees who eventually commit fraud frequently have close ties with their coworkers. In order to manage more tasks with less supervision, they are prepared to put in more hours at work or take fewer vacation days.

Invest in providing your staff with anti-fraud training. There must be proper ethical training for all employees, which teaches them the relevance of ethics and the importance of integrity. They should be aware that it is always unethical to commit fraud or cheat, which helps to change the mindset of those who commit such crimes.

You might also think about setting up a method that allows staff members to anonymously express concerns they may have about possible fraud. Develop a stringent code of ethics that establishes standards for each and every one of your workers.

7. *Protect credit card data*

Credit card fraud has escalated as businesses have become increasingly cashless, particularly in the wake of the COVID-19 outbreak. Actually, the most prevalent kind of fraud worldwide is credit card fraud. It's critical to keep personal and company accounts separate, especially for small firms. Combining business and personal cash exposes you to costly mistakes as well as the possibility of financial loss in the event of fraud.

When paying bills online, use secure services and exercise caution about regarding the parties to whom you give your credit card information.

8. *Robust fraud deterrence system*

There must be a strong fraud deterrence system so that employees do not even think of committing fraud because of its substantial consequences. Employees will refrain from engaging in fraudulent activities because they fear the consequences of fraud, such as losing their jobs and being unable to find employment elsewhere.

Check: How to protect yourself from fraudsters?

Follow these fraud prevention tips to keep your accounts safe from scammers.

- **Near real-time credit monitoring:** Monitor all your bank and credit accounts (including your credit report) for suspicious activity.
- **Account monitoring:** Keep vigilant if your online accounts have been compromised.
- **Malware protection:** Keep all your devices safe from hackers and malware with proper encryption and Wi-Fi protection.
- **Credit lock:** Secure your credit report from unwanted access by locking your financial reports.

References

1. The Economist. 2010. *Taking away Dell's cookie jar.* Available at: http://www.economist.com/blogs/newsbook/2010/07/dells_sec_settlement (accessed on 24 October, 2016)
2. Goel, Sandeep. 2018. Ethical Accounting: The Drver in Recovering Markets, *Eurasian Business Perspectives, Eurasian Studies in Business and Economics* 10/1, Proceedings of the 22nd Eurasia Business and Economics Society Conference, pp. 95–106, Springer. https://doi.org/10.1007/978-3-030-11872-3_7
3. Goel, Sandeep. 2012. Financial reporting–the old age tussle between legality and quality in context of earnings management, *Procedia Economics and Finance*, 3(1), pp. 576–581. https://doi.org/10.1016/S2212-5671(12)00198-0

3 Fraud risk management

Concept, process, and system

Globally, fraud risk management has grown to be a major concern for corporations and regulators alike. Today, every company in the world has taken significant steps to prevent and detect corporate frauds early on. Frauds have a detrimental effect on the organization's long-term viability and public image. In the long run, it could easily bring down the company and have a significant impact on the economy. Fraud risk management (FRM) is the process of recognizing, comprehending, and addressing fraud risks within an organization. It entails creating a programme to identify, stop, and/or prevent both internal and external fraud for an organization. Needless to say, proactive fraud risk management is far more cost-effective than allowing preventable fraud to occur and then spending valuable resources in identifying, investigating, and correcting the consequences.

Fraud risk management system

Fraud risk management system is *the framework of principles based on established guidelines that lay down the structural framework in an organization for combating fraud*. The framework of policies, procedures, and practices that regulate a company's management of fraud risk is known as "fraud risk governance." Corporate governance facilitates both internal and external efforts to prevent and respond to acts of fraud against your business.

A robust and clear policy for managing fraud risk deters potential scammers by highlighting top management's commitment to minimizing and controlling fraud risk. A fraud risk governance policy may contain the following components:

DOI: 10.4324/9781003730224-3

i. imparting staff the knowledge of fraud.
ii. ensuring standards and processes are in place for fraud risk assessment.
iii. continuous fraud risk monitoring.
iv. implementing technology to mitigate and prevent external fraud.
v. provisioning of necessary steps to investigate fraud.

Every component of a fraud risk governance system should be clearly defined, assigned, and accessible, for good governance. In recent years, there have been skyrocketing levels of fraud, enabled by the accelerated adoption of digital commerce and the ever-increasing sophistication of fraudsters. This surge has led to increased fraud-related losses and has damaged customers' experience and trust. Across the industries—from traditional manufacturing and construction industries, as well as in governments, to banking, financial services and insurance (BFSI), e-commerce, and telecommunications—managers must find new ways to fight the ever-evolving threats of fraud while maintaining the highest standards of customer service and opening up new business opportunities.

Fraud risk management—The rationale!

An effective fraud risk management system reduces the risk of theft, corruption, conspiracy, embezzlement, money laundering, extortion, bribery, and other forms of fraud. It also fixes security flaws that allow different threats and application security risks to infiltrate your business.

Fraud risk management is a systematic approach to reducing fraud in an organization. For fraud to be identified early on, an organization should have a fraud risk management procedure. A well-executed fraud risk management procedure can significantly lower fraud rates. Following the detection of fraudulent activity, appropriate and necessary measures must be taken to address it. In short, there shall be an anti-fraud programme in an organization to stop fraudulent activity before it starts.

There are many ways for fraudsters to commit fraud owing to modern technology. Although technological advancements may help businesses manage their fraud risk, it is a fact that these developments also present opportunities for scammers. According to PWC's 2022 Global Economic Crime and Fraud Survey, 46% of the companies surveyed reported they have dealt with fraud cases during the previous two years, as presented in Figure 3.1. Over 1200 CEOs from 53 different countries and regions took part in the poll.[1]

The impact of fraud on stakeholders

Fraud has far-reaching ramifications that are extensive and extend far beyond the perpetrators. These include investors, employees, and the industry as a whole. These parties are frequently the ones who suffer the most from fraudulent activity; they may lose their jobs, have their trust damaged, or incur financial losses. For instance, investors might experience a significant decline in the value of their investments, potentially leading to substantial losses. Employees may be fired or have their professional

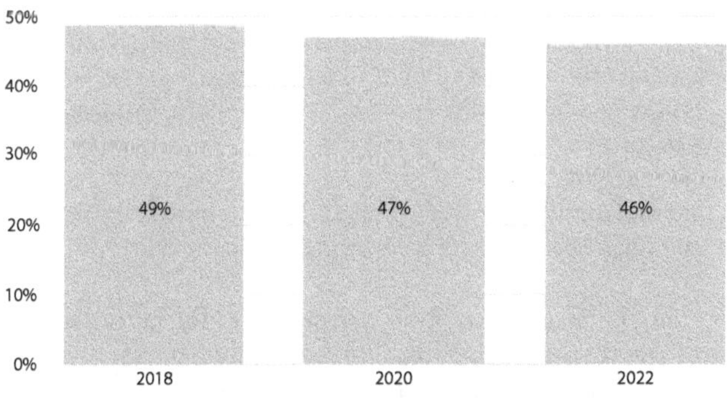

Figure 3.1 Global economic crime and fraud survey—2023

reputation damaged, which could eventually hurt their chances of finding employment. The industry as a whole may suffer from increased regulatory scrutiny and a drop in public trust, which could lead to less investment and unstable markets.

> *Thus, fraud risk management system is crucial for the stakeholders' interests at large. It is imperative that regulators and companies alike comprehend the possible ramifications of fraud on the sector as they collaborate to establish an ethical and transparent financial environment that fosters stability and confidence.*

Process of fraud risk management

It consists of the following steps:

1. **Fraud risk governance**

For evaluating the risk at the right interval, fraud risk management needs to be ingrained in your organization's culture. Stakeholders need to be aware of the seriousness of the fraud risk and willing to accept new procedures. *Fraud risk governance is a framework encompassing the structure of rules, practices, and processes that forms the basis of fraud risk management.*

A strong fraud management plan will probably consist of the following:

- a well-defined plan for senior management and a fraud risk manager to inform and uphold regulations;
- assigning duties and creating detailed job descriptions;
- well drafted procedures for reporting and whistleblowing mechanisms;
- internal auditing procedures and quality control;
- investigations and necessary remedial measures.

There should be necessary tools and strategies for raising awareness of fraud so that investigation and evaluation for preventing and mitigating frauds can be done in a timely manner. These should also be easily available to all team members for the required use.

2. **Identification of fraud risk**

Fraud risk assessment is the process of identifying risks and categorizing them based on their likelihood and impact. A company can provide a clear risk quadrant through the evaluation of fraud risk, which helps leadership choose the best course of action for each type of risk. You can gain a better understanding of your entity's fraud exposure, related risks, and the effectiveness of your current controls by conducting a thorough fraud risk assessment.

Once you know the exact nature of the potential fraud, you can make an accurate assessment of your risk and risk appetite. If you have a clear and specific understanding of your entity's fraud risks, you are in a better position to make necessary adjustments to corporate processes or to amend policy and programme design.

The fraud risk assessment process should be both evidence-based and creative. Those completing the assessment need to be aware of known fraud methods in order to identify how they would do it.

There are four ways that can be used to estimate fraud risk:

- *Recognize the main risks.* Understand which fraud risks pose the greatest threat to your business. Using methods like workshops, brainstorming sessions, seminars, conferences, and comparisons with other businesses in your sector, you may identify the biggest risks.
- *Examine the existing controls.* Analyze your control systems in place for managing fraud risk to find out to what extent they function. This will help discover potential frauds. Regular and comprehensive reviews of all fraud measures are a must.
- *Determine the weaknesses and threats.* You need to identify the other potential weaker areas in the organization. Risks that don't seem dangerous sometimes can stillhave a big impact. For instance, businesses must prioritize preventing online fraud in addition to offline fraud.

- *Integrate fraud risk plan.* There should be no departmental silos in a corporation. In order to guarantee that all departments are in agreement with fraud, you need to have open communication, constructive criticism, and set a good example.

3. Prevention of fraud

After drafting a fraud risk governance strategy and evaluating the fraud risks within your company, you must put in place the policies, controls, and processes necessary to stop (or lessen the likelihood of) fraud.

"An ounce of prevention is worth a pound of cure." This adage certainly holds true when it comes to fraud risk management. Having the right controls and procedures in place can help organizations stop multiple types of fraud before they even knock at the door. For example, handling delayed accounts before they become bad is an ideal example of how organizations can keep themselves safe.

Reduce the three components of the fraud triangle as much as possible in the following ways:

(a) *Motivation:* What monetary rewards are there for persons who commit fraud?
(b) *Rationalization:* What is the justification behind someone defrauding your business?
(c) *Opportunity:* How easy is it for someone to commit fraud without being caught?

Investing in technical fraud prevention tools for online frauds and maintaining sound internal controls for offline frauds is becoming crucial now.

4. Risk detection mechanism

Preventing fraud completely is impossible, no matter how hard you try. Mechanisms for detecting fraud risk are necessary for businesses to prevent fraud before it causes harm. Reporting procedures—like periodic reporting, data mining, trend analysis, etc.—that keep an eye out for anomalies are necessary.

There should be a simple and convenient method for staff members to report fraud.

5. **Risk reporting and monitoring**

Fraud detection might place an innocent worker in a challenging situation. There are a number of reasons why fraud may be unreported:

(i) fear of losing the job;
(ii) failing to recognize the fraud;
(iii) being unsure of how to file a report, etc.

To promote open participation and combat whistleblowing silence, your organization must provide fraud education, an anonymous line of communication, and an open and transparent culture. There should be regular internal and external audits to ensure that your fraud rules and controls are functioning as intended or as your business grows and changes.

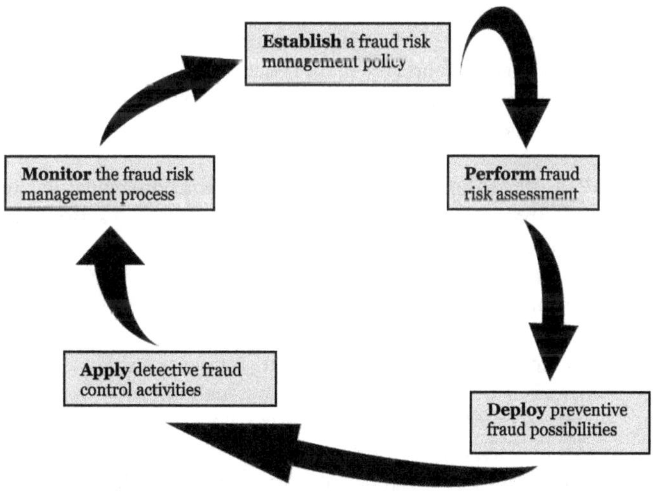

Figure 3.2 Fraud risk management process

The above fraud risk management process is represented in the following Figure 3.2.

Essentials of fraud risk management system

Inarguably, a robust fraud risk management framework can help companies both anticipate and address the risk of various types of fraud. Senior officials and management have a critical role to play in implementing effective anti-fraud measures in corporate organizations. To create an effective framework, there are following prerequisites on which businesses must focus:

1. **Support from the top:** To ensure the holistic adoption of the framework, it is important that leadership is actively involved in both the development and implementation process. Further, at all organizational levels, leadership should ensure that employees' roles and responsibilities are well-defined and that regular checks and balances are in place.
2. **Developing a fraud management strategy:** The strategy should be well aligned with the company's overall strategic goals. It should be comprehensive and adequately balance maximizing the customer experience with attempting to reduce losses through preventive mitigation strategies. Developing a fraud risk plan, procedures, and guidelines, as well as maintaining a strong internal control environment within the organization is another well recognized anti-fraud deterrence measure.
3. **Well-defined operating model:** Organizations must make sure that fraud prevention, detection, and reaction are executed smoothly in order to move away from a reactive approach to fraud and towards a proactive one. To do this, they must match their operating model to the overall fraud risk management strategy.
4. **Detailed fraud risk assessment:** It is crucial to identify and focus on the major, recurring, and high-impact fraud risks because fraud threats vary in their vulnerabilities and impact levels. This can be accomplished through comprehensive and continuous assessments of the fraud risk, which identify weaker points of specific fraud types and provide guidance on the appropriateness of the actions taken to lower these risks.

5. **Better information quality:** There is an urgent need to create a holistic ecosystem that allows businesses to exchange data and information—such as details about fraudulent claims, the history of specific accounts, a list of dishonest businesses and professionals, etc.—in an easy-to-use manner while ensuring the privacy of people's rights.
6. **Effective detection of suspected fraud:** Companies ought to simulate particular circumstances, which, if materialized, would indicate a higher risk of fraud. Fraud at all levels, involving intermediaries, dealers, payrolls, and settlements ought to be covered. The channels should be streamlined in a manner to quickly collect data to conduct further investigation and adopt remedial measures.
7. **Responsiveness to fraud:** Organizations need to develop a well-defined policy outlining the steps involved in looking into and resolving fraud cases. The policy should outline steps for maintaining records and obtaining proof, as well as emphasize who is responsible for what—individuals or departments—depending on the type and severity of fraud.

   The industry participants need to be aware of and take proactive measures to combat fraud, particularly in light of the changing environment and emerging new threats.
8. **Strong ethical culture:** Having a clear code of ethics that has been communicated effectively to all employees, as well as implementing regular training in ethics and an organizational code of conduct, is a necessity. These could increase people's knowledge of anti-fraud policies and procedures and encourage them to report any problems. To make sure that all relevant information has been disclosed, conflict of interest statements can also be used.

The "4Ts" Approach

Fraud risks are uncertain, and they may happen at any time; therefore, it is important to understand that the fraud risks may have pervasive impacts on the objectives and profitability of the organization.

A good way to be responsive to fraud risks is the *4Ts* of risk management:

- Tolerate
- Terminate
- Treat
- Transfer

Tolerate: In cases when the likelihood and impact of the fraud risk are low, then organizations may adopt an easy attitude to the fraud risk because they are within acceptable limits. However, the management should always be ready for informed decisions.

Terminate: Some fraud risks may be outside the fraud risk appetite limits or have a potential severe impact on the organization that might hinder operations. For example, organizations may have to discontinue a business activity in a particular region or country.

Treat: Organizations may decide to take action on the most severe fraud risks to reduce the likelihood or the severity of the fraud risks. For example, installing a firewall to reduce the likelihood of an external intrusion to the application system.

Transfer: Organizations transfer fraud risks by entering into insurance arrangements. For instance, the cash management function of the company may be insured so that, if the fraud occurs and cash is embezzled, the organization may be compensated for the loss.

Best practices for fraud risk management

On average, organizations lose a sizeable percent of their annual revenue to fraud each year. Common risk management practices are often insufficient when it comes to preventing fraud. As a result, companies are turning to fraud risk management to protect their bottom line and meet their risk compliance objectives.

As regulatory compliance increases, it is critical to understand where your organization is vulnerable and establish the appropriate risk management framework to identify and respond to fraud. Organizations need to eliminate unnecessary complexity from the top to bottom and look for incremental approaches for continuous upgradation.

1. *Adequate risk culture*

Risk awareness can help organizations make better management decisions immediately. They must take a methodical approach to incorporating risk awareness and continuous adherence into their financial and non-financial processes in order to maximize the long-term benefits.

2. *Right technology*

Technology can expedite the process of achieving advanced stages of risk managment capabilities. Success would be ensured by integrated and simplified risk management systems. Risk management workflows that are automated and optimized for greater efficiency also foster insights and collaboration.

3. *Compliance aptitude*

Strong compliance benefits the company and the business as a whole. Executives in business must assess where their company stands on the compliance model. A comprehensive understanding of the journey can help organizations decide on the best course of action and the best conditions for progress.

4. *Analytical ability*

Finance professionals need to improve their analytical and detection skills because fraud events of a financial nature are becoming more frequent on both traditional and novel channels, like social media. Organizations need to make the maximum use of the data that is currently available to them in order to improve their ability to manage fraud risk. You need a risk management system that can expand and adjust to new channels because the challenges have become more complex.

5. *Data consolidation*

Businesses need to make sure that data is connected to a single platform for analysis and decision-making from all vendors for better fraud detection capabilities. This will prevent the creation of data silos, which are vulnerable to fraud.

6. *Digitization*

In order to provide an all-round approach to fraud detection, organizations must incorporate all digital channels into their fraud risk management strategy. This reduces the possibility that a fraudster will just switch channels after being blocked on another. Creating a single, centralized platform enables cross-channel correlation of data points and behavioural patterns.

7. *Customer experience*

The degree of risk associated with the transaction must be assessed and controlled before the customer reaches the payment stage. Risk management leaders must create a fraud risk management system that can assess risk at the very beginning of the customer journey. Analyzing activity, assessing the risk of an action, keeping an eye on account creation or login, and determining whether bots or scripts are being used are all part of this. Additionally, they have to set up appropriate barriers based on the level of risk that has been assessed.

8. *Reducing the cost of fraud*

Prior to developing a successful fraud detection strategy, firms need to determine the true cost of fraud to their enterprise. This will enable informed discussions regarding how to best align an organization's goals with a fraud strategy and how much funding should be set aside for fraud detection and prevention. The primary goal of the fraud detection strategy should be to lower the total cost of fraud.

Reference

1. PWC's Global Economic Crime and Fraud Survey, 27/11/2023. https://www.formica.ai/blog/fraud-risk-management#blog

4 Corporate governance

The essence of fraud risk management

The idea of sound corporate governance has gained attention once more since the collapse of Silicon Valley Bank in the US in 2023. India has had its own story of corporate frauds such as Satyam, Kingfisher, ABG Shipyard, and many more over the past two decades. The topic of corporate governance has become an essence of compliance, rather than a mere point of discussion over coffee tables. It has moved from being a taboo subject to becoming a mainstream one, now present in both the political and corporate spheres worldwide. In addition to being significant from a legal standpoint, corporate governance is particularly significant from the standpoint of stakeholders' values. From a firm's perspective, corporate governance ought to be viewed as a practice rather than a requirement.

Concept of corporate governance

Corporate governance is concerned with the standards of behaviour and conduct expected from directors and other senior executives (including the financial manager) in directing and controlling the affairs of a company. Corporate governance not only defines the relationships between managers and shareholders but also includes the relationships between the board, senior executives, shareholders, other stakeholders such as customers, suppliers and employees, regulators, and the firm's auditors.

DOI: 10.4324/9781003730224-4

The simplest of definitions of corporate governance is provided by the Cadbury Report (UK): "*Corporate governance is the system by which businesses are directed and controlled.*"[1]

The Organisation for Economic Co-operation and Development (OECD) Principles of Corporate Governance states:

> *Corporate governance involves a set of relationships between a company's management, its board, its shareholders, and other stakeholders. Corporate governance also provides the structure through which the objectives of the company are set, and the means of attaining those objectives and monitoring performance are determined.*[2]

The Securities and Exchange Board of India (SEBI) (2003) states, "The aim of good corporate governance is to enhance the long-term value of the company for its shareholders and all other partners. Corporate governance integrates all the participants involved in a process, which is economic, and at the same time social."[3]

Corporate governance in India has been influenced by Anglo-American practices. However, the issue in the Indian corporate sector is distinct, as it mainly concerns protecting minority shareholders and disciplining promoter shareholders. The one who has always been overlooked is the ordinary shareholder. However, the landscape is shifting as a result of deregulation, disintermediation, and globalization. Minority shareholders are becoming more powerful and aware of their potential, which is forcing businesses to implement improved governance procedures.

Need for corporate governance

The necessity for having sound corporate governance arises because of the following factors:

1. **Efficient allocation of resources.** The efficient allocation of scarce economic resources is a priority. This can be achieved

if companies are accountable to those who take profits or bear losses after all other claims on the company have been met.

2. **Democratic favour to shareholders.** Today, a large number of shareholders of the company are spread all over the nation and even the world. A majority of shareholders are unorganized and have an indifferent attitude towards corporate affairs. In such a scenario, it is necessary that shareholders' democracy is properly implemented through a code of conduct of corporate governance.
3. **Shareholders' trust.** Corporate scams (or fraud) in recent years have shaken public confidence in corporate management. The need for corporate governance is, thus, imperative for maintaining investors' confidence in the corporate sector.
4. **Societal expectations.** Society today holds greater expectations of the corporate sector in terms of reasonable price, better quality, environmental contribution, and so forth. To meet social expectations, there is a need for a code of corporate governance for the company in economic and social terms.
5. **Sound growth.** For long-term, quality growth, it is necessary that boards of the companies carry out the affairs of the management of the company and monitor development with good corporate governance practices.
6. **Globalization.** The globalization of the economy has driven the largest companies to access international capital markets. Frauds on a global scale have led to greater awareness of inadequacies in governance and demand for reform in corporate practices.

Principles of corporate governance

The key fundamental principles of corporate governance are described as follows.

Transparency

Transparency means the "quality of something" that enables one to understand the truth easily. In the context of corporate governance, it implies an accurate, adequate, and timely disclosure of relevant information about the operating results and other information of the corporate enterprise to the stakeholders.

In fact, transparency is the foundation of corporate governance, as it helps develop a high level of public confidence in the corporate sector. To ensure transparency in corporate management, a company should publish relevant information about corporate affairs in a timely manner.

Accountability

Accountability is the liability to explain the results of one's decisions taken in the interest of others. In the context of corporate governance, accountability implies the responsibility of the chairman, the board of directors, and the chief executive for the use of the company's resources (over which they have authority) in the best interest of the company and its stakeholders.

Independence

Good corporate governance requires independence on the part of the top management of the corporation; that is, the board of directors must be free from all biases so that they can take all corporate decisions objectively.

OECD principles of corporate governance

Originally developed by the OECD in 1999 and then updated in 2004, the 2015 revision of the Principles of Corporate Governance addresses these and other emerging issues that are increasingly relevant. These Principles provide an indispensable and globally recognized benchmark for assessing and improving corporate governance.

The Principles have been adopted as one of the Financial Stability Board's key standards for sound financial systems and have been used by the World Bank Group in more than 60 country reviews worldwide. They also serve as the basis for the guidelines on corporate governance of banks issued by the Basel Committee on Banking Supervision.[4]

These are:

I. *Ensuring the basis for an effective corporate governance framework*
II. *The rights and equitable treatment of shareholders and key ownership functions*
III. *Institutional investors, stock markets, and other intermediaries*
IV. *Disclosure and transparency*
V. *The responsibilities of the board*
VI. *Sustainability and resilience*[5]

Regulation of corporate governance

International

US

The US is known for its shareholder-oriented or market-based model of corporate governance, with features like *active institutional investors, an open market for corporate control, independent outside directors on the board, long-term equity-based compensation for executives*, and *gatekeepers who monitor the process of market disclosure*.

However, scandals like Enron in 2000 generated criticism and led to substantial changes in corporate regulation through the "Sarbanes-Oxley" (SOX) legislation.

The Sarbanes-Oxley Act of 2002 (SOX) introduced major changes to the regulation of financial practices and corporate governance to protect investors from the possibility of fraudulent accounting activities by corporations.

In 1992, the Committee of Sponsoring Organizations of the Treadway Commission (COSO) published its *Internal*

Control—Integrated Framework (the original framework). The framework was widely acknowledged as a pre-eminent framework for internal control design, implementation, administration, and evaluation, as well as for assessing the effectiveness of internal control. COSO revised the original framework in 2013 (COSO 2013 IC Framework). It incorporated 17 principles and made it clear that, for an effective internal control system, each of these principles must be present, functioning, and operating together in an integrated manner. One important principle focused on "fraud risk supervision."[6]

UK

The first version of the UK Corporate Governance Code (the Code) was produced in 1992 by the "Cadbury Committee." In 2012, it was released as the new Code, which applies to all listed companies regardless of whether they are incorporated in the UK or elsewhere.

Presently, the corporate governance model in the UK is based on the *UK Corporate Governance Code* 2018. This market-based approach is basically a system of "comply or explain" (UK Corporate Governance Code) and allows the board to be flexible. The UK Corporate Governance Code is a set of principles of good corporate governance aimed at companies listed on the London Stock Exchange.

It sets standards of good practice in relation to board leadership and effectiveness, remuneration, accountability, and relations with shareholders.

India

Corporate governance was initially guided by Clause 49 of the Listing Agreement before the introduction of the Companies Act of 2013. As per the new provision, the Securities and Exchange Board of India (SEBI) has also approved amendments to the Listing Agreement to improve transparency in transactions of listed companies and give a bigger say to minority stakeholders in influencing the decisions of management. These amendments became effective in 2015.

The corporate governance framework in India has evolved over the years as follows:

1. **Desirable Code of Corporate Governance—Voluntary Code by CII (1998)**

Corporate governance in India gained prominence in the wake of liberalization during the 1990s and was introduced by the industry association, Confederation of Indian Industry (CII), as a voluntary measure to be adopted by Indian companies. The first major initiative was undertaken by the CII in 1998 in the form of the *Desirable Code of Corporate Governance—Voluntary Code.*

2. **The Kumar Mangalam Birla Committee Report (2000)**

Consequently, the second major corporate governance initiative in the country was undertaken by SEBI. In early 1999, it set up a committee under Kumar Mangalam Birla to promote and raise the standards of good corporate governance. *In early 2000, the SEBI board ratified the key recommendations of the Birla Committee, which were incorporated into Clause 49 of the Listing Agreement of the Stock Exchanges.* It soon acquired mandatory status in the early 2000s, through the introduction of Clause 49 of the Listing Agreement, as all prescribed companies listed on stock exchanges were required to comply with these norms.

3. **The Naresh Chandra Committee Report (2002)**

The Naresh Chandra Committee was appointed in August 2002 by the Department of Company Affairs (DCA) under the Ministry of Finance and Company Affairs to examine various corporate governance issues. The Committee submitted its report in December 2002. It made recommendations in terms of two key aspects of corporate governance: *financial and non-financial disclosures, and independent auditing and board oversight of management.*

4. **The N. R. Narayana Murthy Committee Report (Second Report of the SEBI Committee) (2003)**

With an objective to improving corporate governance standards in India, SEBI once again constituted a committee in 2002 under the chairmanship of N. R. Narayana Murthy to review the existing code on corporate governance. Some of the major recommendations of the committee primarily related to audit committees, audit reports, independent directors, related party transactions, risk management, directorships and director compensation, codes of conduct and financial disclosures.

5. Dr J. J. Irani Committee Report (2005)

India's corporate governance reform efforts did not cease after the adoption of Clause 49. In parallel, the review and redrafting of the Companies Act, 1956 was taken up by the Ministry of Corporate Affairs (MCA). The government constituted an Expert Committee on Company Law under the chairmanship of Dr J. J. Irani on 2 December 2004 to offer advice on a new Companies Bill. Based, among other things, on the recommendations of the Irani Committee, the Government of India introduced the Companies Bill, 2008, in the Indian Parliament to introduce the best international corporate practices that foster entrepreneurship and investment. *This finally became the Companies Act, 2013.*

6. Kotak Committee Report (Third Report of the SEBI Committee) (2017)

SEBI set up a committee on corporate governance in June 2017 under the chairmanship of Mr Uday Kotak with a view to enhancing the standards of corporate governance of listed entities in India.

On 28 March 2018, SEBI approved many Kotak recommendations on corporate governance. The recommendations accepted without modification included "reduction in maximum number of listed entity directorships from ten to eight, expanding the eligibility criteria for independent directors, and mandatory disclosure of consolidated quarterly results with effect from 2019–20."

The Indian legal framework has, by and large, been in consonance with the international best practices of corporate governance. Broadly speaking, the corporate governance mechanism for companies in India is regulated by the following regulations.

1. The Companies Act, 2013

The Companies Act, 2013 ("New Companies Act"), replaces the erstwhile Companies Act, 1956 with its applicability still in place. The Companies Act is the principal legislation governing companies in India. It contains provisions relating to board constitution, board meetings, board processes, independent directors, general meetings, audit committees, related party transactions, disclosure requirements in financial statements, and so forth.

The New Act covers corporate governance through the following provisions:

- Companies should have an adequate composition of the boards of directors.
- Every company is required to appoint one resident director on its board.
- The New Companies Act, for the first time, codifies the duties of directors.
- Listed companies and certain other public companies are required to appoint at least one woman director on its board.
- A class action suit was introduced for minority shareholders.

The New Companies Act mandates the following committees to be constituted by the board for prescribed classes of companies:

- *Audit committee*
- *Nomination and remuneration committee*
- *Stakeholders' relationship committee*
- *Corporate social responsibility committee*

Corporate social responsibility (CSR) obligations

India is the only country in the world with codified corporate social responsibility (CSR) obligations. The Companies Act, 2013 requires specified companies to spend at least 2% of the average net profits made during the three immediately preceding financial years on prescribed CSR activities. This provision operates on a "comply or explain" basis, and the board of directors must provide an explanation in the directors' report if the company does not spend the requisite amount on CSR.

This requirement is applicable to companies that have:

(i) A net worth of at least Rs. 5 billion during any financial year
(ii) A turnover of at least Rs. 10 billion during any financial year
(iii) A net profit of at least Rs. 50 million during any financial year.

Every company that fulfils the above threshold requirements must constitute a corporate social responsibility committee, formulate a CSR policy, and make recommendations on CSR to the board. The CSR activities must be performed within India and are not permitted to be for the exclusive benefit of the company's employees or their family members.

2. SEBI's Listing Obligations and Disclosure Requirements (LODR) Regulations, 2015

Presently, the Corporate Governance framework for Listed Companies in India is governed by SEBI (LODR) Regulations, 2015 as amended from time to time. It replaced the governance regime under Clause 49. In addition, companies are also bound by the standard listing agreement of BSE/NSE.

Revised Clause 49: SEBI is a regulatory authority having jurisdiction over listed companies and which issues regulations, rules and guidelines to companies to ensure protection of investors. *SEBI has amended the Listing Agreement with effect from 1 October 2014 to align it with the New*

Companies Act. Revised Clause 49 (2014) and the First Clause 49 (2005) of the Listing Agreement can be said to be a bold initiative towards strengthening corporate governance among the listed companies. This clause intends to put a check on the activities of companies in order to save the interest of the shareholders.

Broadly, **the above regulations** of corporate governance provide for the following:

1. **Board of directors**

The board of directors shall have an optimum combination of executive and non-executive directors with not less than 50% of the board of directors comprising non-executive directors.

(a) Where the *chairman* of the board is a *non-executive director*, at least one-third of the board should comprise independent directors, and in case the *chairman is an executive director*, at least half of the board should comprise independent directors.
(b) If the non-executive chairman is a promoter of the company or is related to any promoter or person occupying management positions at the board level or at one level below the board, at least one-half of the board of the company shall consist of independent directors of such number of minimum independent directors, as prescribed.

Independent directors

Independent director is any non-executive director who possesses relevant expertise and integrity and in no way is related to the company.

2. **Audit Committee**

The audit committee to be set up comprises a minimum of three directors as members, two-thirds of whom shall be independent.

3. **Disclosure requirements**

Periodical disclosures relating to the financial and commercial transactions, remuneration of directors and so forth need to be done by the company to ensure transparency.

4. **CEO/CFO certification**

The CEO and the CFO shall certify to the board that they have reviewed the financial statements and that they are fair and in compliance with the laws/regulations and accept responsibility for internal control systems.

5. **Report and compliance**

A separate section in the annual report should be on "compliance with corporate governance." Also, a quarterly compliance report needs to be submitted to the stock exchange signed by the compliance officer or CEO.

The corporate governance norms in the country have been strengthened by the Companies Act, 2013, and the Listing Obligations and Disclosure Requirements (LODR) Regulations 2015 of the Securities Exchange Board of India (SEBI) for listed companies. The key emphasis is placed on "fraud" by recognizing it as a key risk and the Board of Directors and the senior management are held accountable for effective risk management. In the case of listed entities, there is an additional safeguard by the "Audit Committee" which consists of independent directors on the board of directors who perform the necessary checks and take proactive steps to mitigate risk.

References

1. Report of the Committee on the Financial Aspects of Corporate Governance. 1992. December, www.ecgi.org/codes/documents/cadbury.pdf (accessed on 5 October, 2016).
2. OECD. 2004. *OECD Principles of Corporate Governance*, www.oecd.org/corporate/ca/corporategovernanceprinciples/31557724.pdf (accessed on 5 October, 2016).
3. SEBI. 2003. 'Report of the Committee on Corporate Governance', 8 February.
4. OECD. 2016. *'G20/OECD Principles of Corporate Governance'*, www.oecd.org/ corporate/principles-corporate-governance.htm (accessed on 5 October, 2016).
5. OECD Library. 2023. *'G20/OECD Principles of Corporate Governance'*, https://www.oecd-ilibrary.org/docserver/ed750b30-en.pdf?expires=1696151552&id=id&accname=guest&checksum=FC18A0E0C3AABE920D5CD1A1A4809B4D (accessed on 1 October, 2023).
6. Fraud Risk Management Guide, Second Edition. 2023. COSO, March. https://www.acfe.com/fraud-resources/fraud-risk-tools---coso/fraud-risk-management-guide

5 Management compensation
Economic value added (EVA)

"Value creation" is the ultimate objective of any corporate organization. The most successful organizations understand that the purpose of any business is to create value for its customers, employees, investors, and, most importantly, its shareholders. The management of companies needs to take their incentives on economic value rather than accounting profit, which is subject to greater manipulation. This provides the basis for a comprehensive and integrated *value-based management compensation system* that not only helps in evaluating business performance for all the stakeholders but also enables the management in fair business conduct.

Value-based compensation!

"Value creation" is a corporation's **raison d'être**[1], the ultimate measure for fair managerial compensation. Debate has focused on what is the most appropriate type of "value-based compensation" for the corporation to distribute. Is it:

- *The compensation linked to the value of the company in the stock market (its market value)?*
- *The compensation linked to the value shown in its balance sheet (the accounting or book value of its assets minus its liabilities)?*
- *The compensation linked to value based on its expected future performance—profits or cash?*
- *None of these?*

DOI: 10.4324/9781003730224-5

> From the governance perspective, value-based compensation implies a business distributing managerial compensation when earning revenue more than expenses, that is, when its return on capital exceeds the cost of capital.

Economic value added (EVA): The shareholders' value-based compensation

The shareholders are the most important stakeholders of a company, as they are the owners of the company. *Therefore, the main emphasis of the management is on creating "real" value for shareholders and thereby taking the compensation.*

Traditional compensation measures

Traditional approaches to managerial incentives are based on "shareholders' value creation," using parameters such as *earnings capitalization, market capitalization, and others.*

1. Market price

In the 1990s, the measure that was prominently used for analyzing shareholder value was the "company's market price." The presumption was that shareholders look for capital gains from their investments. But the measure based on stock market value is subject to the same wild fluctuations as the market itself. In a rising tide, all boats are raised. But when macroeconomic changes force up markets, it does not mean that the value of every company in that market rises. The markets are moved by sentiment that has little to do with the underlying value of individual corporations.[2]

2. Earnings per share (EPS)

The limitation of market value, as discussed above, was evident in the form of the dotcom frenzy at the end of the 1990s. So, a group of scholars favoured "earnings per share" (EPS) as the real measure of shareholders' value. But the accounting measures are not carved in stone. They can (and do) differ from country to country and have their own set of accounting limitations. They are not free from the biases of management.

Economic value added (EVA) compensation measure

A measure developed to overcome these problems is called EVA (economic value added). It is the professedly managed innovation in the field of internal and external performance measurement for "management incentives." Stern Stewart, a UK-based consulting firm, unveiled EVA (economic value added) in the year 1990, but its origin as economic profit dates back to the early 1900s. *EVA is the financial performance measure that captures the true economic profit of an enterprise.* This is the reason why EVA has been successfully employed in nearly 400 companies worldwide, including well-known firms such as Coca-Cola, Siemens, and Sony.[3]

EVA computation!

This is the measure of output (taken as operating profit after tax and some other adjustments) less input (taken as the annual charge on the total capital employed, including both debt and equity). In simple terms, EVA is the profit generated by an economic entity in excess of its cost of capital. If the difference between the above two parameters is positive, then the entity is said to be creating wealth for its stakeholders. A negative EVA, on the other hand, indicates the company is a destroyer of value.[4]

EVA = Net Operating Profit after Tax (NOPAT)—Cost of Capital Employed (COCE)*

Where *NOPAT* is the profit generated from the core operations of the company.

* "Cost of Capital Employed" is also referred to as weighted average cost of capital (WACC).

It is calculated as: Profit before tax + Non-operating items (including Interest) − Tax.

Cost of Capital Employed is calculated as: Weighted average cost of debt and equity (WACC) × Average capital employed. It is the total invested capital in the business.

Thus, the real test of the management is to generate returns higher than the investment from core activities for shareholders' wealth maximization. According to Mr. Roberto Goizueta, the former chairman and CEO of the Coca-Cola Company and an ardent believer in the maximization of shareholders' wealth: *"Management doesn't get paid to make shareholders comfortable. We get paid to make the shareholders rich."*[5]

Example: How is value created?

Young India Company (YIC) is a leading software company in India. In the year 2023, YIC's net assets generated pre-tax operating profits of INR 240 million, as reported in its income statement. The corporate tax rate is 30%.

The company employed INR 1,000 million of capital as shown in the balance sheet for 31 March 2023. YIC's weighted average cost of capital (WACC) is 10%.

EVA = Net Operating Profit after Tax (NOPAT) – Weighted Average Cost of Capital

NOPAT = INR 240 million – INR 72 million (30% tax amount)
= INR 168 million

WACC = INR 100 million (10% × INR 1,000 million)

So, EVA = INR 168 million – INR 100 million
= INR 68 million

YIC generated INR 168 million of after-tax operating profit (NOPAT) but consumed INR 100 million of funds in the process. Therefore, YIC generated a positive EVA of INR 68 million in the year 2023. As long as YIC keeps generating positive EVA, it will create value.

How to grow EVA?

EVA will increase if:

(a) Operating profits are increased with less capital; that is, greater efficiency in the use of resources is present.
(b) Return on capital invested in additional projects is more than the cost of obtaining new capital; that is, profitable growth is achieved.
(c) Capital is used in activities that cover the cost of capital; that is, productive use is achieved.

Case: EVA of Hindustan Unilever Limited (Sector—FMCG)

Hindustan Unilever Limited (HUL) is a leading fast-moving consumer goods (FMCG) company in India. It is a nearly 100-year-old company in the sector in India with brands like Dove, Lux, Lipton, and Lifebuoy among others.

The company has been following EVA for years. At HUL, the goal of sustainable long-term value creation for its shareholders is well understood by all the business groups. This can be seen in Table 5.1 and Figure 5.1.

Calculation of COCE

1 *Cost of debt* is taken at the effective rate of interest applicable to a "AAA" rated company like HUL for a short-term debt, net of taxes. They have considered a pre-tax rate of 6.43% for 2021–22 (6.28% for 2020–21).
2 *Cost of equity* is the return expected by the investors to compensate them for the variability in returns caused by fluctuating earnings and share prices.

Table 5.1 EVA reporting of HUL

Particulars	*2017–18*	*2018–19*	*2019–20*	*2020–21*	*2021–22* (*Rs. in crores*)
Cost of Capital Employed (COCE)					
1. Average Debt	0	0	0	0	0
2. Average Equity	6,181	6,668	7,227	46,890	**47,156**
3. Average Capital Employed: [1] + [2]	6,181	6,668	7,227	46,890	**47,156**
4. Cost of Debt, post-tax %	5.21	5.77	5.25	4.7	**4.81**
5. Cost of Equity %	14.19	11.84	9.11	8.86	**9.09**
6. Weighted Average Cost of Capital % [WACC]	14.19	11.84	9.11	8.86	**9.09**
7. COCE: [3] × [6]	877	789	658	4,153	**4,289**
Economic Value Added (EVA)					
8. Profit After Tax (PAT), before exceptional items	5,135	**6,080**	**6,743**	7,963	8,724
9. Add: Interest, After Taxes	0	0	0	0	0
10. Net Operating Profits After Taxes [NOPAT]	5,135	6,080	6,743	7,963	8,724
11. COCE, as per [7] above	877	789	658	4,153	4,289
12 EVA: [10]—[11]	**4,258**	**5,291**	**6,085**	**3,810**	**4,435**

Source: Hindustan Unilever Limited. 2022. 'Economic Value Added', Annual Report 2021–22, https://www.hul.co.in/files/92ui5egz/production/8a1b3f103408328781a6ebf434b8e5172e4bfc91.pdf (accessed on 26 September 2023).
Note: Rs. (INR) 1 crore = Rs. 10 million.

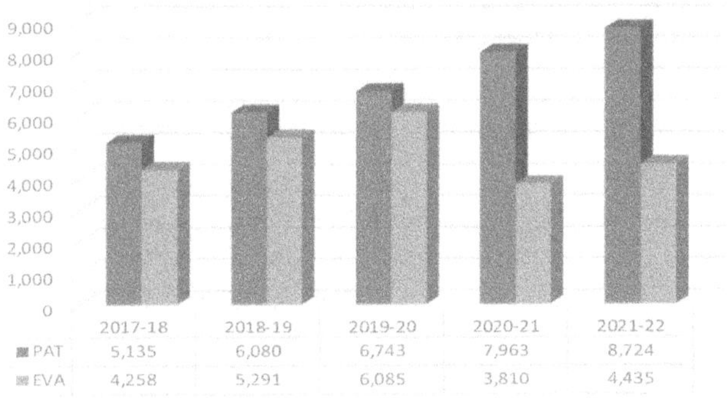

Figure 5.1 EVA trend of HUL

Note: Rs. (INR) in crores.

Cost of equity = Risk-free return equivalent to yield on long-term government bonds (taken at 6.84% for 2021–22).

+

Market risk premium (taken at 3.68%) × Beta variant for the Company (taken at 0.614), where Beta is a relative measure of risk associated with the Company's shares as against the market as a whole.

Thus, HUL's cost of equity = 6.84% + 3.68% × 0.614 = 9.09%

ANALYSIS

HUL has shown considerable improvement in EVA (from INR 4,258 crores in 2018 to INR 6,085 crores in 2020, with a decline in 2021 due to known external factors. In 2022, it again showed an increasing trend.). The company has been able to bring down the cost of capital (COCE) significantly in 2019 and 2020 and then maintain a steady increase to become a zero-debt company, thereby improving EVA performance.

Therefore, the difference between Profit after Tax (PAT) and EVA is not very huge except during the past two years, a positive sign for the shareholders.

How to measure value creation? Market value added (MVA)

As known, the core objective of financial management is "value creation." This means that before making a business decision, managers should always ask themselves the key question: *will the decision raise the value of their firm?*

The key question can be answered with the help of the fundamental finance principle: "when the return on invested capital exceeds the cost of capital," that is "EVA."

EVA and growth

Goel (2012) found that the companies in India that were reporting positive EVA from 2004 to 2009 had grown at a much faster pace compared to SENSEX vis-à-vis the companies reporting negative EVA.

The companies which were not reporting EVA had underperformed with respect to SENSEX.[6]

MVA framework!

EVA is directly linked to the growth of the company, and that is expressed by "market value added" (MVA). If MVA is positive, the firm is creating real value because the market value of its capital exceeds the amount of capital invested in it. If MVA is negative, the firm is destroying value.

The real measure of determining the value of a company is EVA with positive MVA. To find out whether management has created or destroyed value as of a particular point in time, the *market value* of the firm is compared with its total capital (both equity and debt capital) to the amount of capital that shareholders have invested in the firm (the firm's capital employed).

Market value added (MVA) = Market value of capital – Capital employed

Example: EVA vs. MVA

Considering the earlier example of Young India Company, a leading software company in India, let us understand the implication of MVA. The company employed INR 1,000 million of capital as shown in the balance sheet for 31 March 2023. It consisted of INR 700 million of equity and INR 300 million of debt. The market value of that capital as on the date was INR 1,500 million.

MVA = Market value of capital—Capital employed
= INR 1,500 million – INR 1,000 million
= INR 500 million

So, MVA is positive with INR 500 million, indicating that YIC has created INR 500 million of real value as of 31 March 2023, with a positive EVA of INR 68 million.

How to estimate the market value of capital?

(i) *For publicly listed companies*: The market value of capital can be obtained from the financial markets, at least for firms whose equity and debt capital are publicly traded in the form of securities.

(ii) *For private companies*: If the firm is not publicly traded, its market value is unobservable and its MVA is difficult to calculate. It can be calculated based on its estimated purchase price, that is, if someone makes an offer to buy the firm, then it could be taken based on that "offer price."

References

1. The Economist. 2009. *Value Creation, 'The Ultimate Measure By Which a Company Is Judged'*, 20 November, www.economist.com/node/14301714# (accessed on 5 September, 2016).

2. The Economist. 2009. *Value Creation, 'The Ultimate Measure By Which a Company Is Judged'*, 20 November, www.economist.com/node/14301714# (accessed on 5 September, 2016).
3. Goel, Sandeep. 2012. EVA reporting in India: The market analogy, *Singapore Management Review*, 34 (2): 18–29.
4. Goel, Sandeep. 2012. EVA reporting in India: The market analogy, *Singapore Management Review*, 34 (2): 18–29.
5. Shapiro, A. 1990. *Modern Corporate Finance*. Basingstoke: The Macmillan Company, p. 333.
6. Goel, Sandeep. 2012. EVA reporting in India: The market analogy, *Singapore Management Review*, 34 (2): 18–29.

6 Industry interface of fraud risk management structure

With an increasing number of customers in the Indian industrial sector, there is a rise in the risk of fraud. In an effort to attract customers, corporates, including banks, insurance providers, fintech firms, and traditional consumer and allied producers, have been experimenting with various value propositions. The need for fraud monitoring and control is also growing as companies and their clientele grow. The intentional use of false or misleading information by con artists to illegally obtain funds, property, or legal rights from another person or organization is on an expansion. Despite the fact that laws expressly address fraud and prosecute, and punish the offenders under specific sections that address fraud-related offences like forgery, fraud, and cheating, the problem persists.

Fraud risk management in the BFSI sector

The Banking, Financial Services and Insurance (BFSI) sector is poised to grow multifold as the domestic economy moves ahead in its journey to emerge as a developed economy by 2047. Fraud risk in BFSI has been a cause of great concern to stakeholders due to sporadic risk management practices among entities and a lack of adequate financial and digital literacy. The growth of BFSI is sure to follow as the economy expands. India has the potential to reach US$ 26 trillion by 2047. Logically, BFSI is set to rise tenfold in asset size during the period. Hence, the sector has to be ready to mitigate fraud risk in light of the increase in businesses in geometric progression.[1]

Every year, businesses in the retail and financial services industries lose billions of dollars to data breaches and fraud, and the threat of future incidents continues to escalate. In financial

DOI: 10.4324/9781003730224-6

services, 25% of companies lost over $1 million to fraud last year.[2]

The architecture for fraud risk management needs to be systematically strengthened in order to protect the BFSI sector. It is noteworthy that the BFSI is increasingly using AI and data science to automate various processes and enhance user experience. Business processes driven by AI and cognitive analytics, blockchain, cybersecurity, and the metaverse have the potential to produce best-in-class BFSI services. Other future industry drivers include customer centricity, regulatory scrutiny, fintech partnerships, and central bank digital currency (CBDC) with an emphasis on environmental, social, and governance (ESG). In addition to preparing to provide a multichannel customer experience, the BFSI sector has witnessed digital applications across the entire company value chain and has been monitoring new opportunities presented by emerging competitors. Fraudsters are well challenged by the standard-setters and policy-makers in this boom.

According to Insurance Regulatory and Development Authority of India (IRDAI) regulations, all insurance companies must have a "Fraud Monitoring Framework." Protections against, detection of, prevention of, and mitigation of the risk of fraud by intermediaries, employees of insurance companies, and policyholders/claimants must all be included in the framework. Insurers are expected to employ a comprehensive strategy to identify, quantify, control, and monitor fraud risk as well as to implement appropriate risk management policies and procedures. Every year and at any other time that may be considered necessary, the boards of insurance companies are required by the IRDAI to review each company's specific anti-fraud policy.

The RBI provides banks with guidance on how to design and put into place an appropriate framework for managing fraud risk, which covers all the steps involved in identifying, assessing, mitigating, monitoring, and informing higher management about fraud, as well as on how early detection and treatment should be implemented. An effective fraud risk management strategy can significantly lower the total costs of fraud for a bank.

"Operational risk" includes the management of fraud risk. Although BFSI firms and consumers adhere to the regulatory systemic measures required for operational risk, fraudsters take advantage of them because they lack the necessary skills and expertise to foil their schemes. The following actions should be taken:

(i) putting operational controls in place;
(ii) reporting attempted frauds;
(iii) gathering loss data;
(iv) training staff and developing their abilities;
(v) educating customers on "Dos and Don'ts;" and
(vi) putting whistleblower procedures into place.

Building process controls in a granular way, while aiming for ease of doing business, can help achieve two objectives of the fraud risk management framework: *lowering the overall cost of fraud and fostering a risk-aware ecosystem*. Regardless of the source, it will enable improved anticipation, identification, prevention, and management of fraud risk.

The discussions clearly indicate: (i) BFSI's increasing potential for growth due to its enlarged product line and related issues; (ii) Operational risk, vulnerability, and fraud risk all rise with increased reliance on technology; and (iii) The wider user base might lack the expertise needed to address fraud issues.

The BFSI sector must create a precisely calibrated framework for managing fraud risk in light of these clear indications of increasing fraud threats.

Observing the early warning signals (EWS)

Corporate lenders can benefit from early warning signals since they can identify potential fraud and notify the relevant parties beforehand. As an illustration, the following could be early warning signs of fraud or financial misappropriation:

- Suspicious use of corporate assets, including the creation of shell corporations;
- Unusual spikes or patterns in money movement, like circular transactions between group corporation accounts;
- The excess inventory is out of line with sales; and
- Recurring mistakes and discrepancies in invoices and payments.

Early warning indicators, such as a request for money transfers to a party other than the company's regular raw material suppliers, can help businesses spot potentially fraudulent transactions before they occur. No matter how big or small the fraud, they can also identify patterns, such as the gradual siphoning of funds through the inflation of invoice pricing.

Modern technology-enabled fraud monitoring systems use state-of-the-art technologies like big data, natural language processing (NLP), and artificial intelligence/machine learning (AI/ML) to identify patterns in past and current data and alert authorities before more damage is done. Most businesses lack comprehensive or integrated fraud control systems, making them a prime target for scammers.

Fraud monitoring systems need to be able to identify anomalies quickly and provide recommendations for possible fraud sources. The secret to this is a culture of continuous improvement that integrates corporate machinery and technology, while ensuring the involvement of all stakeholders.

Fraud risk management in the public sector

Large corporate scandals and frauds have shaken both the private and public sectors over the past few decades. These scams have serious negative effects that are hard to measure and quantify. They are not widely publicized because of their frequently detrimental effects on an organization's finances and reputation. Most of the frauds are hard to detect. They are still only unintentionally discovered after continuing for extended periods of time, even with improved fraud prevention and detection techniques. A growing regulatory environment and the global rise in fraud occurrences have prompted governments and organizations to step up their efforts to combat fraud risks.

When it comes to fraud in the public sector, issues such as bribery, corruption, and misuse of authority during public procurement often come into the picture. These practices usually involve misuse of entrusted power for personal gain, often including cash given "under the table," which leaves very little or no financial statement evidence that a crime has occurred. Such crimes are uncovered in most cases through tips or complaints from third parties, often via a fraud helpline, or are detected during internal reviews, external audits, and by financial inspections.

Frauds within the public sector, including State-Owned Enterprises (SOEs), originate from both internal and external sources. These frauds can be committed by any employee at any level within the organization. They can range from small-scale abuse of travel expenses to large-scale frauds involving high-value contracts and breaches of controls that could have serious and material consequences. Examples of other fraud and illegal activities include money laundering (the transforming of profits of crime and corruption into legitimate assets), tax evasion (the deliberate reporting of false information in tax reporting), and informality (economic activity that is not taxed or monitored by governments).

The best method for public sector organizations to reduce these frauds is to have strong internal controls, which include maintaining a strong internal control environment. However, even a robust internal control framework cannot ensure that fraud won't occur in an organization. It is therefore critical to implement additional lines of defence, such as an effective and efficient internal audit function. In addition to fostering best practices guidance for creating successful fraud management programmes, emerging technologies, particularly the application of data analytics, can help internal audits in preventing and detecting fraud.

The "who," "how," and "where" of fraud risk management

Understanding markets, counterparties, and the forces that could upend a company's agreements and presumptions has always been essential to mitigating business risk. Since Covid-19, there has been an unprecedented level of corporate risk, with businesses juggling the effects of the pandemic with threats from all directions. Responding to emerging threats and attempting to stay ahead of them while still combating established risks are the main goals of risk management today. The ubiquity of newer risks is different from that of older ones. Do Indian businesses suffer from similar levels of persistence? Adding urgency to these new risks is the need to establish appropriate systems and capabilities for combating them. The key notable advancements of FRM post-pandemic which have happened for the future, obviously the good, can be discussed below.[3]

1. Board-level engagement

Fraud risk is lower in internal business cultures that value transparency and accountability as best practices. Senior leaders play a key role in integrating this ideology throughout an organization by setting a good example at the top, aligning performance goals with moral behaviour expectations, and continuing to mentor employees to help them navigate challenging circumstances. It is encouraging that more attention is being paid to bribery and corruption in the boardroom.

There still seems to be a major disconnect between head office expectations and the local business practices in regional offices or supplier chains, even though board members are apparently paying more attention to these concerns. In order to close this gap and lessen the chance of fraud, there is a need for a top-down focus on long-term cultural messaging. Organizations must go beyond basic compliance guidelines for this task.

2. Enterprise-risk assessment and internal controls

The majority of sources state that, in order to identify possible risks to their operations, businesses have conducted enterprise-wide risk assessments during the past couple of years. Firms worldwide have demonstrated a greater level of confidence in the ability of their internal control systems to detect and thwart high-risk fraud activity. On average, three out of four companies believe their internal control system is effective. This is true across all industries and business sizes.

However, it's crucial to keep in mind that the only way to build confidence in a control framework is through ongoing testing. Furthermore, if the human elements of the chain are not adequately managed, educated, or otherwise equipped to take action, non-compliance and illegal activity will continue and go unreported even with the strongest compliance systems in place on paper. Organizations must perform regular risk assessments, third-party audits, and proactive analysis utilizing a combination of internal and external data in order to identify hazards early. Effective frameworks must ensure that the control environment is adaptable enough to change with the times.

3. Third-party risk management

Given the challenges corporates face with third-party risk, the majority of businesses are not making full use of data collection and analytics as part of their ongoing third-party due diligence to provide adequate assurance over these elements. If businesses want to take control of both internal and external threats, they must come up with innovative ways to obtain reliable and timely on-the-ground information in every location where they conduct business.

In order to identify irregularities in their global supply chains, as well as at their headquarters and satellite offices, they must employ advanced information analysis techniques. They will be better able to understand their industry and the risk profile that goes along with it. Only by bridging the gap between the C-suite, local business practices, and third parties with such an approach can organizations effectively address the risk of frauds in their operations.

4. Cybercrime cushion

Cybercrime has evolved over the last few decades from an IT issue to a boardroom problem, reflecting the global economy and the digital transformation of corporate operations at both the micro and macro levels. The more the business sector integrates digital elements, the more likely it is that technology has become, or will become, a conduit for criminal activity. Furthermore, criminals still commit crimes in fields where cybersecurity breaches are prevalent. For example, there is a high risk that cyber breaches would lead to intellectual property theft, internal information leaks, and data theft.

It follows that, unlike so many other silos, cybersecurity must be part of an organization's overall risk management strategy. This emphasizes how important it is for businesses to maintain appropriate data governance in accordance with their risk profile.

Strategy for fraud risk management

An effective strategy for fraud risk management involves a pragmatic approach to identify, mitigate, and prevent the occurrences of fraud based on an organization-wide awareness programme imbibed in the culture itself.

The three key determinants of an effective strategy for fraud risk management are given below:

Organizational culture

- Conducting surveys to find out how well informed employees are about the organization's ethical cultural values.
- Training programmes for existing and new employees on fraud awareness.
- Periodic evaluation of the efficiency of the whistleblowing mechanisms in place.

Application of technology

- Use of forensic analytics tools and techniques to identify and flag suspicious transaction trends and patterns.
- Utilizing information technology software to gather evidence on identified fraud incidents.

Organizational control

- Independent fraud investigation upon receiving preliminary evidence.
- Organizing training and orientation workshops for fraud sensitization among employees.

References

1. https://timesofindia.indiatimes.com/blogs/kembai-speaks/fraud-risk-management-in-bfsi-sector/ (accessed on 18 February, 2023)
2. https://www.pingidentity.com/en/resources/blog/post/fraud-mitigation.html (accessed on April 11, 2024)
3. https://www.mycii.in/KmResourceApplication/77474.CIIKrollIndiaFraudSurveyReportDigitalFinal7Oct21.pdf

7 Global frauds

The rationale for pursuing fraud risk management, as indicated in the literature, is supported by case evidence(s) of corporate frauds globally. It identifies the culprits and their circumstances based on the "driving actions" behind fraud, where others may have surely helped it. This is the beginning of the story of the rotting apples. "Charles Ponzi, an Italian con man and businessman who lived life to the fullest until his imprisonment, is ultimately responsible for the ideation of these schemes. His most well-known creation, the 'Ponzi Scheme,' saw him swindle thousands of investors out of about $32 million in the early 1920s—an amount that would now be valued at nearly half a trillion dollars." There are more such models of gullible managers and traders in the digital era, providing a wider landscape for scammers.

WorldCom (2002)

WorldCom was a telecom provider in the United States. Over the course of its $11 billion asset inflation, the telecom behemoth caused investors to lose $180 billion and resulted in the loss of 30,000 jobs. The CEO, Bernie Ebbers, was found to have inflated revenues through false accounting entries and underreported line costs by capitalizing expenditures rather than reducing them. He was sentenced to 25 years in prison for conspiracy, fraud, and the submission of false paperwork. The controller resigned, the CFO lost his job, and the company filed for bankruptcy. In January 2006, Verizon Communications acquired WorldCom, which is now known as MCI.

"It was a leadership issue." *Therefore, the board of directors should closely examine people and make sure they are qualified before they join the C-suite.* For a CEO, don't take an

DOI: 10.4324/9781003730224-7

inexperienced person. Essentially, the business plan would rely on constant growth and stock values. A conscientious CEO would never permit such actions.

Enron (2002)

Enron, an American energy company, was found to have utilized "mark-to-market accounting." Based in Houston, the company provided energy, commodities, and services while maintaining large loans off its balance sheets. The company filed for Chapter 11 bankruptcy, which cost investors $74 billion, in addition to the retirement plans and jobs of thousands of workers.

Prior to the fraud's discovery in 2001, the company's main financial ploys were creating fictitious special purpose entities (SPEs), generating virtual profits, and winning over the markets with substantial payments to banks and analysts. Enron reported $20 billion in total revenues in 1997; that amount had multiplied fivefold to $101 billion by 2000! With yearly fees topping $52 million, auditor Arthur Andersen played a big part in the company as an auditor and consultant.

Senior executive Sherron Watkins raised the alarm when speculation of wrongdoing was stoked by soaring stock prices. Jeff Skilling, the CEO, received a 24-year prison sentence. Kenneth Lay, the chairman, died before he could be sentenced to prison. Upon pleading guilty to two conspiracy counts, going to prison, and losing $24 million, former CFO Andrew Fastow was the one running the fraudulent ship and pocketing at least $30 million in "fees" through SPEs.

Parmalat (2003)

Like many frauds, the Parmalat scam started out as an attempt to conceal losses. CEO Calisto Tanzi decided to falsify financial documents to hide the division's losses from the public when the company's South American division started to lose money in 1990. Parmalat's decision to commit fraud made the firm route reliant, as is the case with many frauds, and this in turn encouraged ever-more dishonest accounting methods and self-dealing. Despite having over €4 billion in cash and equivalents on its balance sheet, Parmalat's 2003 €150 million bond issue failed, and this is when the scam was eventually uncovered.

On a family-run farm in Northern Italy, Parmalat was established in 1961. In the years that followed, the business progressively expanded into a global conglomerate and became well-known as one of the biggest dairy and food businesses in Italy. Parmalat identified 214 firms in 48 countries during its 2003 crisis.

They increased their revenues over these 13 years, from 1990 to 2003, by creating fictitious transactions by employing a double-billing strategy. With the receivables from these fictitious sales acting as collateral, they obtained more bank loans. They inflated reported assets by fabricating fictitious ones. Financial engineering strategies included, for example, declaring sales as $6.77 billion when they are actually $5.04 billion, and displaying net debt as $2.29 billion while the exact amount is $18.0 billion. On 27 December 2003, Parmalat was formally declared bankrupt, and CEO Calisto Tanzi was arrested on fraud-related charges. In 2005, Parmalat was relisted on the Milan Stock Exchange.

Lehman Brothers (2008)

This financial services company had a sizeable portion of its debt liabilities hidden away as an off-balance-sheet entity. It filed for bankruptcy due to its unethical practices, which involved passing off debts totalling more than $50 billion as sales.

It was a team effort with numerous complex causes. To put it briefly, Lehman was too liquid and had insufficient collateral to be able to renew the repurchase agreement contracts (repos) or borrow enough money from the Federal Reserve to keep things from collapsing. Essentially, it was borrowing money for a short period of time from the future to make the necessary corrections the next quarter, and so on. Lehman was a perfect example of reporting an extra $20 million. It was supposed to be a one-time steal from the future that was made up for in the next quarter, but it continued.

Satyam (2009)

A total of INR 50,400 million in false cash and bank balances, INR 3,760 million in non-existent accrued interest, INR 12,300 million in understated liabilities, and INR 21,610 million in exaggerated receivables contributed to the $1.5 billion inflation in earnings of Satyam, a global software company based in India that was found to have falsified employee and customer identities in order to overestimate profits and cash balances.

Ramalinga Raju, the company's founder and chairman, wrote a letter to the board of directors acknowledging the deception. He and his brother were accused of conspiracy, cheating, record-faking, and breach of trust. He then claimed that the situation had gotten out of control and likened it to "riding a tiger, not knowing how to get off without being eaten." In 2009, the Mahindra Group eventually bought Satyam.

Kingfisher (2012)

Even with all of his accomplishments, Vijay Mallya is most remembered for the scandal that followed the downfall of Kingfisher Airlines. Kingfisher became well known shortly after its founding in 2005, due to remodelled aircraft, friendly airline staff, delicious cuisine, and—most importantly—an excellent in-flight experience in 2006. Kingfisher Airlines was one of the biggest scandals that hurt India's economy.

In addition to the money laundering and fraud charges brought against him, Vijay Mallya continued to run his aircraft firm by taking out bank loans totalling INR 90,000 million from 17 banks, and other banks continued to give him credit even after SBI declared him bankrupt. His business also collected employee income tax, PF, and traveller transport tax; however, he did not share these figures with the IT or PF staff. The company was forced into bankruptcy due to its inability to pay staff salaries.

Kingfisher's financial problems led to the airline's closure in 2012; in December of that year, its operating permit was revoked; additionally, Vijay Mallya ceased fulfilling his obligations. By this time, the Kingfisher corporation was almost out of business. The main reason for the airline disaster was poor leadership; there was never a permanent CEO or MD at Kingfisher.

Toshiba (2015)

Known for producing computers and gadgets for both home and business use, the Toshiba firm was taken private by a group led by Japan Industrial Partners (JIP) on December 20, 2023, marking the end of its existence as a publicly traded firm.

After revealing accounting irregularities involving multiple businesses and senior management in 2015, Toshiba was found to have overstated pre-tax earnings by 230 billion yen ($1.59 billion) over the course of seven years. In January 2020, additional accounting errors were discovered at a fully owned subsidiary, and in July 2020, an annual general meeting rejected the nominations of five activist shareholders for directors.

On 25 June 2021, the board's shareholders removed board chairman Osamu Nagayama, citing the board's purported inability to address claims that it had put pressure on investors. Toshiba had promised to engage with prospective investors and conduct a thorough asset appraisal. In November 2021, Toshiba announced that it would divide into three companies: an energy company, an infrastructure company, and a management company for its interest in Kioxia. Osamu Nagayama, the chairman of the board, was dismissed by the shareholders for allegedly not carrying out his responsibilities.

PNB (2018)

Punjab National Bank (PNB), which involved a substantial sum of about INR 150,000 million, was the first significant financial fraud to be disclosed in the nation. Nirav Modi and Mehul Choksi perpetrated the fraud (via Choksi's listed firm, Gitanjali Gems). They were both involved in the import and export of raw and polished diamonds. Both had developed retail diamond networks over time in India and at well-known foreign locations. Nobody questioned Nirav's financial source at the time. Only a few years later did this extraordinary deception come to light, shocking the country like never before.

With the help of a few junior level banking officials, Nirav Modi scammed PNB and other banks by opening enormous amounts of letters of credit (LC) with no underlying transactions—basically, paper money. He took advantage of a simple flaw in the IT systems that prevented LCs from being reconciled with the underlying transactions. Despite the rule that applied to all banks, the LCs that were opened were not reported in the RTGS system. Therefore, until the fraud was discovered, the existence of such LCs was unknown.

There were several warning signs that should have alerted authorities and bank management to the fraud much sooner but were disregarded. The RBI repeatedly sent out red alerts to all banks, directing them to address these systemic weaknesses (primarily RTGC and non-reconciliation). However, these were also ignored.

India is currently making efforts in international courts to get Nirav and Mehul back to India after they were able to flee the country.

IL&FS (2018)

Infrastructure Leasing & Finance Services Limited (IL&FS) was one of India's biggest financial scandals, valued at an estimated INR 990,000 million. This scandal turned the tide against the nation's corporate regulators and accounting advocates. The Institute of Chartered Accountants of India (ICAI), the country's accounting professional association, announced the formation of a committee to investigate IL&FS issues and provide recommendations, and in February 2019, the ICAI released an updated set of codes of ethics. The Ministry of Corporate Affairs of the Government of India also published the "National Guidelines on Responsible Business Conduct" in March 2019.

The primary investment firm and holding company for the IL&FS Group is IL&FS Ltd. The company operated in over a dozen service industry sectors, such as tourism, education, urban infrastructure, and transportation. It looked to be a well-managed business with an informed board of directors.

The entire crisis began when the IL&FS management began taking out loans from a variety of sources, both secured and unsecured. The astronomical and irrational loans obtained from different financiers and investors became an irreversible burden, and they began to default on all debts, loans, and investor deposits overnight. The company's credit ratings declined the day after the rating agencies' deceit was revealed. This problem was discovered in July 2018 when two IL&FS entities, ITNL and IFIN, stopped repaying loans and inter-corporate deposits to specific banks and lenders. Over the following few months, more and more IL&FS Group companies filed for bankruptcy. The IL&FS group's disregard for organizations and regulations entered a new phase.

The directors were accused of financial misappropriation and unlawful income diversion. The government fired the company's senior management and put them in jail just one day after taking office. A new board made up of well-known figures from Indian finance and business was subsequently established.

DHFL (2020)

The first-ever fraud in a home finance organization was Dewan Housing Finance Ltd. (DHFL), which occurred primarily as a result of promoters' direct participation in money laundering and fund siphoning. DHFL and its directors, Kapil Wadhawan, Dheeraj Wadhawan and others, were booked for allegedly defrauding 17 banks of INR 34,615 crore (INR 346,150 million).

Loans were made to people who weren't creditworthy or who weren't well-known and had the same addresses in secret. Approximately six lakh (600,000) phony accounts were created at one bank using the names of borrowers who had already paid back their debts. Loans that were used to divert money to promoter companies were made possible by these accounts. In the end, these debts proved to be unrecoverable. As a result, enormous amounts that were not recoverable were represented as recoverable on the balance sheet.

Silicon Valley Bank (2023)

The abrupt and widely publicized fall of Silicon Valley Bank (SVB) on 10 March 2023, involving the concealment of enormous losses from investors, regulators, and depositors, serves as a stark warning about the dangers corporate fraud poses to the US financial system.

Better risk management and monitoring are plainly needed to prevent corporate fraud, as our findings demonstrate. A proposed class action was filed against SVB, Chief Financial Officer Daniel Beck, and Chief Executive Greg Becker in federal court in San Jose, California.

SVB was the largest bank failure in the US since the 2008 financial crisis, with an estimated $209 billion in assets and $175.4 billion in deposits. The failure has raised concerns about a contagion among other lenders catering to affluent customers, including large regional banks and venture-backed tech start-ups.

Silicon Valley Bank was unique in that it focused on lending money to start-ups in the biopharma and IT industries. Like other banks, it required deposits, but unlike other banks, a significant portion of these deposits came from software businesses with substantial funding. The bank decided to place its depositors' money in secure, long-term Treasury bonds in order to give them a reasonable return on their money. All was well until the Federal Reserve began hiking interest rates significantly, which unfortunately forced the bank to issue long-term, low-interest Treasury bonds in response to pressure to give its depositors higher rates of return as a result of the interest rate hike.

The bank was quickly hit by a liquidity crisis, which occurs when depositors take out more money from banks than the banks can handle. The bank realized it needed to raise more money to

Table 7.1 Corporate Fiasco Portfolio

Company	*Year*	*Country*
WorldCom	2002	US
Enron	2002	US
Parmalat	2003	Italy
Lehman Brothers	2008	US
Satyam	2009	India
Kingfisher	2012	India
Toshiba	2015	Japan
PNB	2018	India
IL&FS	2018	India
DHFL	2020	India
Silicon Valley Bank	2023	US

compensate its depositors, so it filed with the Securities Exchange Commission (SEC). Regretfully, depositors rushed to withdraw their funds, viewing the fundraising effort as additional proof of the bank's insolvency. The bank was eventually acquired by First Citizens Bank on 27 March 2023.

The above descriptive fiascos list is given in Table 7.1.

8 Brainstorming

Supplementary resource

A. "Risk chart"

Both risk—company & transactions

Anti-Money Laundering—AML

Transaction rating	C	A
	• **"Watch list"** accounts • Company risk rating is high, transaction risk rating is low	• **"No issues"** accounts • Company risk rating is low, transaction risk rating is low
	D	B
	• **"Immediate action"** accounts • Company risk rating is high, transaction risk rating is high	• **"Watch list"** accounts • Company risk rating is low, transaction risk rating is high
-10 Company rating	–10	10

For the fraud landscape, to move to PREDICT and PREVENT FRAUD the above process is a valuable tool.

- Collect volume of data with the objective of finding hidden patterns and analyzing relationships between numerous types of data.
- Accounts are plotted on a "risk chart" based on the country risk and the transaction risk rating
  A. Cool map—"Risk chart"
  B. Still cool map—"Risk chart"

DOI: 10.4324/9781003730224-8

C. Feeling warm map—"Risk chart"
D. Hot map—"Risk chart"

B. Tools and techniques—Fraud detection

There is a need for every management to implement an anti-fraud programme. There should be systems and procedures in place within an organization, to allow it to operate efficiently and effectively.

Therefore, the first important tool available is "training and experience." The second tool is the "necessary mindset"—that fraud is always a possibility. After taking fraud into account, the "necessary investigation" is the next course of action.

In addition to the "tools" described above, there are common techniques available to help identify irregularities leading to fraud. Organizations should ensure that resources are allocated to identifying such anomalies and detecting cases of fraud.

- **Background reading:** It is important to keep up to date with fraud trends and issues. You can undertake a fraud risk assessment and detect the significant potential frauds identified through the risk assessment. Act on irregularities that raise a concern.
- **Benchmarking:** Do comparisons of one financial period with another; or the performance of one cost centre, or business unit, with another; or of overall business performance with industry standards. These can highlight anomalies worth further investigation.
- **Systems analysis:** It is important to examine the systems in place and identify any weaknesses that could be opportunities for fraud to occur.
- **Ratio analysis and modelling:** It can be used to identify any abnormal trends or patterns, applying the "sort" tool to identify patterns in expenditure and other items.

C. The Benford's law—Fraud detection model

Benford's law describes the relative frequency distribution of a dataset's leading digits. Smaller leading digit values are more common than larger ones. If all digits were represented equally, then they would each appear one-ninth (about 11.1%) of the time. Yet in an uncanny number of real-world data sets, an astonishing 30.1% of the entries begin with a one, 17.6% begin with a two, and so on. This phenomenon is known as *Benford's law.*

According to this law, approximately 30% of numbers start with a one while less than 5% start with a 9. This law states that leading 1s occur 6.5 times more frequently than leading 9s! Benford's law is also known as the "First Digit Law."

Figure 8.1 displays the distribution of leading digits according to Benford's law.

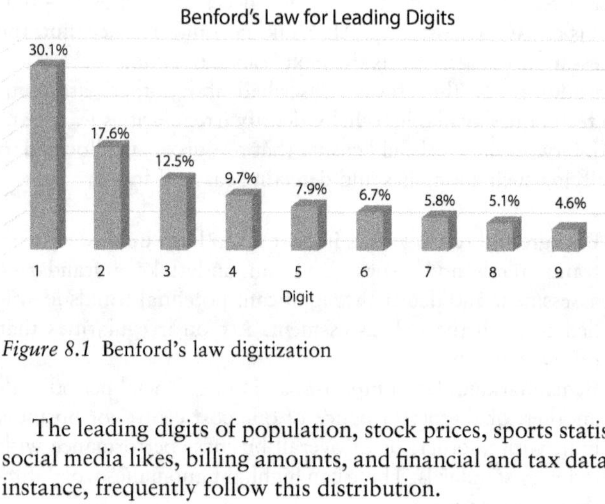

Figure 8.1 Benford's law digitization

The leading digits of population, stock prices, sports statistics, social media likes, billing amounts, and financial and tax data, for instance, frequently follow this distribution.

Use of Benford's law

It has been widely used by analysts to look for "fraud" and "manipulation" in financial records, tax returns, applications, and decision-making documents. They use Benford's law to compare the leading digit distribution in these datasets. *When the leading digits don't follow the distribution, it's a red flag for fraud in some datasets.*

There is a simple explanation for why this works. When people manipulate numbers, they don't track the frequencies of their fake leading digits, producing an unnatural distribution of leading digits. In some cases, they might systematically adjust the leading digits to be below a particular threshold value. For example, if the transaction type has a $100,000 limit, fraudsters might start many numbers with a 9 for $99,000.

> Using Benford's law to find fraud is admissible in local, state, and federal US courts. In the past, it has detected irregularities in Greece's EU application and investment return data for Ponzi schemes, such as Bernie Madoff's.[1]

It works best for data that ranges over multiple orders of magnitudes from extremely low to extremely high. You can cover the 10s, 100s, 1000s, and so on. For instance, population and incomes can vary greatly. *If a dataset that you would expect to follow Benford's curve doesn't, it's just a red flag and not evidence of fraud. However, the auditors and investigators can target dubious records more effectively.*

Benford's law formula:

$$P(d) = \log_{10}\left(1 + \frac{1}{d}\right)$$

Table 8.1 Benford Probability Score

First Digit	*Benford Percent of Occurrence as First Digit (%)*
1	30.10
2	17.61
3	12.49
4	9.69
5	7.92
6	6.69
7	5.80
8	5.12
9	4.58

Where d = the values of the leading digits from 1 to 9.

The formula calculates the probability for each leading digit.

The table below displays the probabilities that Benford's law formula calculates for all digits.

In general, Benford's law applies to data that meet the following criteria:

- *Quantitative data*
- *Larger datasets*
- *Multiple magnitudes, from very low to very high*
- *No restriction of minimums or maximums*
- *Measurable data*

It doesn't apply to assigned data (numbers), such as phone numbers, ID numbers, etc.

Example!

Let's take an empirical example of Benford's law using "Excel."

- We downloaded the sales of a manufacturing sector company, Gen Ltd., in India for 2023–24. Do the leading digits for these sales numbers follow the hypothesized distribution?
- The dataset satisfies the above assumption—multiple orders of magnitudes from extremely low 85 to extremely high 98,657 (in INR). The large *sample* size (n = 1006) makes the data theoretically perfect for this test.
- For using Excel, we need two Excel functions:
  - Left: To get the leading (or other) digit.
  - Countif: To get the counts for each leading digit.
- Figure 8.2 shows the results in graph format with data labels. On the chart, the "Black" line represents the relative frequency of each leading digit observed in the dataset, while the "Grey" line indicates the values that Benford's law predicts.

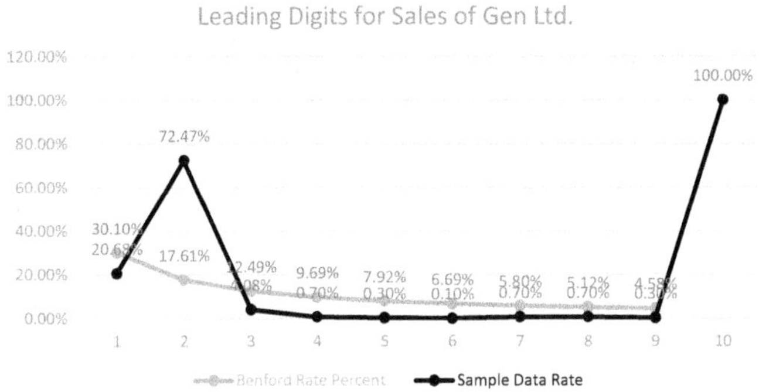

Figure 8.2 Benford's digitization of "Sales" of Gen Ltd.

In summary, it provides evidence that some firms do manipulate and commit frauds when they anticipate reporting a loss, an earnings decline, or falling short of investors' expectations.

D. Fraud prevention policy template

Background

Instilling strong standards of corporate ethics and organizational values is one of ABC Ltd.'s missions.

The board should implement policies and procedures that should include:

(a) Staff responsibilities concerning fraud prevention and identification;
(b) Process of reporting on fraud-related issues to the management;
(c) Accountability of fraud investigation once a fraud has been detected;
(d) Procedures for reporting and documenting fraud allegations; and
(e) Requirements for training on fraud prevention and identification.

Regulations

The above framework shall be in accordance with the Securities and Exchange Board of India (SEBI) guidelines.

Further, every listed business, or any class or classes of companies, as may be prescribed, shall provide a vigil mechanism for directors and staff to report legitimate concerns in any manner that may be prescribed, according to Section 177(9) of the Companies Act, 2013.

According to section 143(12) of the Act, an auditor of a company shall promptly report the matter to the Central Government within the timeframe and in the manner that may be prescribed if, while performing their auditing duties, they have reason to believe that an offence involving fraud is being or has been committed against the company by officers or employees of the company.

The Institute of Chartered Accountants of India (ICAI) has released Auditing and Assurance Standard (AAS) 4, titled "The Auditor's Responsibility to Consider Fraud and Error in an Audit of Financial Statements." It states that "those entrusted with the governance and management of an entity have the primary responsibility for the prevention and detection of fraud and error."

Policy requirement

In keeping with the aforementioned, the public company requires creating the Fraud Prevention Policy as part of the framework for managing fraud risk, expressing the board of directors, audit committee, and senior management's commitment to identifying, preventing, and controlling fraud risk. The goal of the company's fraud risk management framework is to be a crucial component of overall risk management and to be included in the organization's business philosophy, policies, and plans.

Policy

"To defend the company against all forms of fraud that cause loss and harm to the organization's reputation by implementing integrated strategies for successful and efficient fraud prevention, detection, and remediation."

Objectives

The goal of the Fraud Prevention Policy is to establish controls and procedures for identifying, preventing, and detecting fraud, as well as to raise awareness among senior management, employees, business associates, vendors, customers, and others doing business or having dealings with the company of their respective responsibilities for fraud prevention, detection, and reporting.

The policy also seeks to strengthen the overall fraud risk management framework of the organization by promoting an ethical and fraud-free workplace and by fostering a culture that encourages fraud prevention by all the concerned stakeholders.

Actions constituting fraud

The term fraud could have a wide range of coverage such as, but not limited to forgery, bribery, corruption, deception, embezzlement, misappropriation, false representation, concealment of material facts, theft and collusion.

Fraud reporting

Any employee, vendor, contractor, or other third parties doing business with the company is obliged to report the incident(s) as soon as they become aware of any suspected fraud or fraudulent activity. The Nodal Officer(s) will handle this reporting at the Work Centre Level.

The Nodal Officer must report each fraud complaint to the Fraud Risk Management Committee (FRMC) through the Fraud Control Officer (FCO) for review. If necessary, the information must also be sent to the Board, the Audit & Ethics Committee, or both.

When a report of suspected fraud is made, the Nodal Officer and other designated authorities will take every possible step within their power to safeguard the rights and reputations of all parties concerned, including the person who in good faith made the complaint.

ABC Ltd. will handle all information received in relation to a complaint or investigation in confidence. The existence may only be disclosed to those who need to know in order to look into or deal with the situation.

Fraud investigation

FRMC will appoint an investigator who will be in charge of the investigation, based upon the merits of the complaint. The complaint and the subject will be given a chance to be heard during the investigator's investigation.

The investigation must be conducted objectively, without prejudice, and as a neutral process for gathering facts. The investigator assigned to the probe will report to the FRMC through FCO. To guarantee that proper and appropriate action is taken, the pertinent ABC Ltd rules will be adhered to after the investigation is finished.

The FRMC will evaluate the investigation's findings and, based on the importance of the issue, report its conclusions to the Board and the Audit & Ethics Committee.

E. Fraud control plan and strategy

Your fraud control plan documents your entity's key fraud risks and current and planned strategies to fight against fraud.

A good fraud control plan should include the following essentials:

- a statement about your entity's weightings for fraud risk
- an outline of key roles and responsibilities for fraud control within your organization
- an action document of relevant awareness-raising and training strategies
- a summary of how your organization evaluates fraud risk and handles organizational vulnerabilities
- a layout of current strategies and timelines to reduce fraud risk within your organization
- a clear stance on who is responsible for creating, putting into practice, and assessing fraud strategies and procedures
- details on the reporting of suspected frauds
- protocols for reporting fraud incidents
- a summary of how information about fraud incidents is collected, analyzed, and reported

An **example** of what a good **counter-fraud strategy** might look like below.

Step 1: Calculate liabilities

Before starting, you should have a realistic idea of your current fraud situation. You'll need to know how much revenue you have coming in and how much fraud currently costs you.

Your total fraud liability encompasses a lot more than just sales revenue. It would help if you also accounted for:

- Overhead costs like lost merchandise, shipping, interchange, etc.
- Chargeback fees
- The cost of internal resources used for fraud management
- Lost future sales and reputational damage from fraudulent activity

You can map out a projection of your monthly fraud costs:

1. Strategic Fraud Intelligence
   - Oversee and monitor your entity's counter-fraud plan and strategy.
2. Risk Factor Assessment
   - Conduct high-level and functional/programme-level fraud risk assessments to proactively identify vulnerabilities and implement countermeasures.
3. Counter-Fraud Assurance
   - Undertake pressure testing to check that countermeasures are appropriate and work effectively.
4. Fraud Measurement
   - Implement fraud measurement exercises to quantify the extent to which undetected fraud may exist.

Step 2: Establish your risk tolerance level

An acceptable level of risk varies. The situation may be impacted by a number of external factors. For example, merchants in high-risk industries like financing have more built-in risk than retailers in a low-risk vertical. You can conduct research to better understand your industry's typical range of risks.

5. Referrals and Detection

    - Establish procedures and tools for receiving and evaluating tip-offs and identifying possible fraud indicators.

Step 3: Develop a blueprint for fraud risk management

So, the next step is to bring your fraud costs in line with your goals?

You could cut back on spending...but then your fraud levels would likely rise.

What you need is a plan. You have to look at your options, then decide on a strategy and a timeline for implementation.

6. Intelligence and Investigations

    - Set processes to investigate potential fraud.

7. Respond and Disrupt

    - Lay down processes in place to deal with potential fraud, including:
        - referrals for prosecution
        - coordinated disruption activities
        - improving prevention countermeasures.

Step 4: Deploy Fraud Risk Management Strategy

The cornerstone of your strategy must rest on addressing risk management in all of its manifestations. On an internal level, this entails fixing issues with personnel or procedures. A number of tools or tactics can be used to prevent external fraud, some of which you may already be utilizing.

8. Report and Adapt

    - Report on all counter-fraud activities and notify this back to the strategic fraud intelligence resource to modify the strategy.

Step 5: Monitoring, tracking, and reporting

As time goes by, you need to know your plan is working. Your numbers are closer to an acceptable percentage. Without monitoring and reporting, you can't know.

Fraud risk management is an ongoing process. Fraud techniques are constantly evolving, so your strategy will need to be fine-tuned as you go. Utilize the data produced by your fraud prevention tools to continuously refine your approach, identify emerging risks, and enhance your outcomes.

Determine which fraud KPIs are most pertinent to your company, then put procedures in place to gather pertinent information from your daily activities. Continue to keep tabs on fraud cases and performance.

After gathering all of that information, you must create thorough reports that contrast approaches, outcomes, and return on investment. You should regularly review these reports and modify your tactics in light of the data.

Fraud investigation—"Case study"

The background

The company is the UK-based leading multinational having a presence in ten continents and around 100 countries. The core business of the company is in manufacturing and supply of printing paper.

In India, the company started its operations from December 2014 with head office in Delhi and three other branches across India, viz. Mumbai, Kolkata, and Chennai. The company was led by Mr. Clean, who was appointed by the parent company with the objective of looking after India's operations.

Over the period of time, the turnover of the company has increased phenomenally and the same was unparalleled with the growth of the companies in other countries which has raised doubt in the mind of CFO of parent company.

Objective

The CFO hired a professional advisory firm to perform an initial review of the books of accounts in order to assess the Indian subsidiary's internal control system and analyze the accuracy of its operations, ultimately identifying any fraudulent activity within the organization.

Process

- Preliminary inspection of the books of account for two days along with the senior representative from the parent company (the US) was done with the objective of forming an initial opinion on the affairs of the Indian subsidiary.
- On the basis of opinion of the preliminary investigation, it was found suspicious; therefore, in-depth scrutiny was held of all the units of the Indian Subsidiary.
- Above assignment was carried out in detailed phases of planning, compliance and substantive review across business segments, and finally interview and collection of necessary information.

Key findings

- Inflation of sales / turnover to get the performance incentive and later they were recorded as sales returns.
- Non-existence of customer and transactions of Rs. 8 million thereof.
- Receivables' (Debtors') ledger was artificially inflated by Rs. 10 million.
- Unauthorized discount/commission to the customers.
- Bogus inventory reported in Delhi warehouse and transactions thereof.
- Cash amounting Rs. 2 million was withdrawn by the Country MD for his personal benefit by way of personal expenses, which were in excess of his allowable remuneration as per the terms of his appointment letter.

Analysis

(i) The company's business operations lacked internal control governance practices as everything revolves around the country's MD. The internal controls were completely overlooked.
(ii) The Finance Head of the Indian subsidiary has not played the expected roles and acted as a mere facilitator to the Country MD, whereas he should have raised the above red flag.
(iii) The findings clearly indicate that the company in India was a "One Man Show" operation which has led to poor financial indiscipline.

Conclusion

- The company terminates the employment of the Finance Head on the basis of findings and appoints a completely new finance and accounts management team.
- Further, it takes a legal action against the Country MD against fraudulent activities done by him.

Fraud risk management—"Case exercise"

FPT case

FinoT Payment Technology (FPT) is one of the promising Financial Technology Start-Up Companies in India. FPT was founded in 2008 and has emerged as one of the largest players in India's Domestic Money Transfer (DMT) (Cash to Bank) segment. It is an award-winning Online Transaction platform for DMT, Payments and Travel.

FPT has received several honours and awards, including the prestigious National Payments Excellence Award 2019 organized by the National Payment Council of India for the largest number of transactions in the IMPS (non-Bank category). It has one of the largest cash collection network agents in the country to handle cash collection and banking activities.

Amit, the founder of FPT, is now aspiring to apply for the Small Payment Bank Licence next year in 2025. The application has to be made to the Reserve Bank of India (RBI).

As per the banking industry practices, they wish to test the five potential risk scenarios that they would face while operating a small payment bank in India. Accordingly, they will prepare a formal report to adopt the risk scenarios with specific risk management actions to be submitted with the bank licence application to RBI.

Required:

1. Design the top five risk scenarios in the following format out of the risk scenarios given in the exhibits below.

Risk Scenario: Title
Risk Scenario: Type
Risk Scenario: Impact
Risk Scenario: Likelihood Scale
Risk Scenario: Impact
Current Measures to Manage Risks

---

2. Prepare a report to the Board of FPT for "Bucketing" of the above identified risks.

Exhibit 1

Non-compliance—FPT'S own shell

FPT, as a fintech company, like other companies, has a peer-to-peer (P2P) lending platform. P2P lending establishes an instantaneous marketplace for lenders and borrowers to interact and match incoming and outgoing remittances.

For instance, if someone in London wants to send money to India, they can deposit it at the London office of the platform. The platform then "nets" or matches the transaction. Nonetheless, strict adherence to the Banking Regulation Act, RBI Act, Foreign Exchange Management Act (FEMA), 1999, Prevention of Money

Laundering Act, and other laws must be ensured by the compliance function.

The Reserve Bank of India (RBI) will supervise all peer-to-peer lending (P2P) platforms, according to a government announcement from India. The Reserve Bank of India's decision to allow foreign direct investment (FDI) in financial services firms other than banks or insurance companies, but with a risk premium, is advantageous to fintech companies.

Exhibit 2

Cyber-attack on the systems

A recent hack into the system of a PSU Bank resulted in the creation of fake documents that could have been used to raise money outside of India or help sell illegal goods. A letter of credit (LC) or guarantee was a fraudulent document.

The bank later learned that its SWIFT (Society for Worldwide Interbank Financial Telecommunication) system had been used to create fake documents. The bank was sending documents and millions of dollars across borders using the financial messaging service SWIFT.

Exhibit 3

Investment fraud

A major international bank has experienced a 400-million-INR banking fraud. The mastermind behind the scam is an employee by the name of Anil. Selling financial goods to high-net-worth individuals (HNWIs) was Anil's mode of operation. He misrepresented to the HNWIs that the bank's investment product committee had approved these financial instruments.

He therefore deceived them by telling them that their money would be invested in attractive projects that would yield high returns. He then moved the money collected from HNIs to a few bogus accounts. About twenty customers' funds totalling INR 400 million were transferred to these accounts. After that, he invested the money in the stock market.

Exhibit 4

Money laundering channel

ABC Bank was accused of money laundering. It was alleged that 11 fraudulent corporations were used to transfer foreign exchange worth 5570 million INR out of India under the pretence of imports.

Investigations also showed that 66 ABC accounts were managed by a person and his partner. Furthermore, according to bank records, the accused deposited <5050 and had it transferred abroad through this bank between 2012 and 2016.

His illegal money transfers to Hong Kong were justified by fabricated import documents. He was the owner of two Hong Kong companies, CD and YZ. In actuality, funds were moved to these two companies.

Exhibit 5

Nature crisis

Storms, earthquakes, and other extreme weather have a direct impact on small enterprises. Being a small financial technology business, ZEO Payment Technologies got negatively impacted by a natural disaster.

The devastating 2021 flood in Thailand had an impact on practically every industry, including electronics and automobiles, and was felt globally. This led to a lot of businesses outsourcing their supply chain to a few low-cost nations. However, a fintech company's business might also be disrupted.

Figure 8.1 Benford's law digitization

Figure 8.2 Benford's digitization of "Sales" of Gen Ltd.

Reference

1. https://statisticsbyjim .com /probability /benfords -law. Jim Frost.

Glossary

Accountability It is a liability to explain the results of one's decisions taken in the interest of others.

Apparent authority It is the authority that a regular, reasonable citizen can infer from an agent.

Business It is an independent legal entity that is established by a statue or a registration process.

Corporate governance It is the system by which businesses are directed and controlled.

EVA It is the financial performance measure that captures the true economic profit of an enterprise.

External fraud These frauds are from outside of an organization.

Financial statements fraud It occurs when an individual manipulates an organization's financial statements.

Fraud It is an intentional deception that causes the personal or some form of gain of an employee or an entity.

Fraud risk assessment It is the process of identifying risks and categorizing them based on their likelihood and impact.

Fraud risk governance It is the framework of policies, procedures, and practices that regulate a company's management of fraud risk.

Fraud risk management system It is the framework of principles based on established guidelines that lay down the structural framework in an organization for combating the fraud.

Identity theft It refers to any kind of fraud committed by stealing personal information.

Independent director It is any non-executive director who possesses relevant expertise and integrity and in no way is related to the company.

Mortgage fraud It is a wilful misrepresentation or omission of facts by an individual or an organization.

Opportunity It refers to circumstances that make possible fraud to occur.

Pressure It refers to an employee's mindset towards committing fraud.

Rationalization It refers to an individual's justification for committing fraud. Justification is the last stage in the fraud triangle theory.

Real authority It is the authority that a firm has fully granted to its agent or employee.

Tax evasion fraud It is the deliberate use of wrong information in filing income tax returns.

Transparency It means the 'quality of something' which enables one to understand the truth easily.

Wrongful gain It has been defined to mean gain by unlawful means of property to which the person gaining is not legally entitled.

Wrongful loss It has been defined to mean loss by unlawful means of property to which the person losing is legally entitled.

Index

For Product Safety Concerns and Information please contact our EU representative GPSR@taylorandfrancis.com
Taylor & Francis Verlag GmbH, Kaufingerstraße 24, 80331 München, Germany

www.ingramcontent.com/pod-product-compliance
Lightning Source LLC
LaVergne TN
LVHW021131300926
849160LV00010B/972
9781041220213